Achieving Academic Excellence:
How to Study
Second Edition

Happy Studying!

Mark A. Mateyko

i

Archimedes

"Give me a place to stand,
and I will move the earth."

Achieving Academic Excellence:
How to Study
Second Edition

Mark A. Mateya, Esq.

PAMARAM
PUBLISHING
—

Pamaram Publishing
Mark A. Mateya
55 W Church Ave
Carlisle, PA 17013
717.241.6500

It is normal that this page of a book will have two and sometimes three sentences of legal language (in addition to the copyright), often in smaller type, making it as hard to read as it is to understand. No additional disclaimers have any part of this book. If you liked reading these unnecessary sentences, you will really enjoy reading Achieving Academic Excellence; How to Study.

Achieving Academic Excellence: How to Study, The Second Edition
Mark A. Mateya

Includes Index

ISBN 978-1-7322857-0-5

Table of Contents

Foreword

Education is a preparation for life. Lawyer Mark Mateya, now heading his own Law Firm, is convinced that success in any kind of self-fulfilling life requires a Master Plan for achieving it. Early in his book, he candidly confesses he had no plan when he drifted through High School with poor grades and few satisfactions. He was admitted to Penn State after committing himself to academic goals initially, and then to professional goals. He majored in both English Literature and Writing. He found both to be exciting and professionally useful. He graduated summa cum laude. His growing reading, writing, and analytic skills were essential to the career he imagined, but so were his elective courses.

All careers involve people-to-people relationships. Solid relationships require a broad understanding of the human condition – an ability to see one's self in the context of family, community, and even in our inescapable connections to a global economy. All relationships are informed by an awareness of both human history and current events; by a sensitivity to complexities in the human condition revealed in all the arts and sciences; and by a recognition of our own our inner paradoxes. We all yearn to be independent on the one hand and to have a place in some community on the other. Education is a process of making personal sense of all that touches us. Master Plans for education -- and life -- should reflect some coherent ordering of all that. But any useful Master Plan for life must be flexible enough to accommodate inevitable change in response to new learning.

Mateya, in a modest conversational way, looks back at his own discoveries about how to develop an Academic Master Plan. He offers advice about choosing and sequencing both major and elective courses; how to get help from Professors and Advisors;

how to take notes; how to prepare for exams. He notes the values of Study Aids and Study Groups. Much of his advice is common sense. But many people, including students, tend to ignore common sense. They ignore the intellectual discipline required to make even their own provisional sense of the world and the essential values needed to sustain it. Sticking to the priorities that best serve that reasoned vision is even harder to do. The major warning in the book is not to ignore such intellectual discipline.

Mateya tells students how best to get help from teachers, advisors, and other administrative support systems in pursuing their dreams. But his greater message is that only the student has the ultimate responsibility to figure out what major to choose or change. Accepting such responsibility is, indeed, hard work. It takes courage also to engage in continuous self-examination, and to give priority to what is most likely to achieve ultimate goals. Students are even responsible for their teachers. It is up to them to figure out what every teacher -- exciting or not -- has to offer that might help validate his or her current views -- or significantly, and perhaps even wonderfully, change them.

Mark asked me to write this forward to his book. He had been a first-rate student of mine in a Shakespreare course a long time ago. I was a fairly young man then. I am now in my 83rd year. I am astonished and gratified that he should remember me. I can now take some pride in his book. I think his message goes beyond other "how to study" books. It is a challenging application of "critical thinking," to achieving both academic and professional success.

Judd Arnold
Emeritus Associate Professor of English,
The Pennsylvania State University
State College, PA

Acknowledgements

There are a host of people who made it possible for me to write this book. I would like to thank them for their assistance, without whom this book would not have been possible.

Nancy Hayward, my first college English professor, who convinced me that I was smart enough to be a good college student. (Ms. Hayward—you can send me the corrected version of my book at your convenience.)

My wife Ramona, without whom I would not have been able to tackle this project. Her support and the support of my family has been invaluable.

Betsy Roumm, my friend who helped me write this tome the first time through. A good friend is hard to find. Janelle French, my copy editor this second time through. Her honest edits helped keep me on track.

Roy Spancake and Paul Yeager whose enthusiasm for this project was matched only by their creativity in making everything look good!

Professor Emeritus Judd Arnold who inspired me to be a good writer and a good lawyer long before law school.

Introduction

"The most reliable way
to predict the future is
to create it."
Abraham Lincoln

I decided to write this book after taking time to reflect on my own experiences in higher education. I graduated from high school with poor grades, barely passing my senior English class. I went on to major in English and Writing in college and graduated summa cum laude. I learned study skills and other lessons along the way that made the difference for me. I want to pass these lessons on to you. I believe that you can become a better student by mastering these same skills. You picked up this book because you hope that there are studying techniques and skills that can be learned, and you are right.

No matter how well you have done in school, you can improve your grades by improving your learning and studying skills. This book will assist you by providing you with tools to help you focus on what is important and teach you how to use your time wisely.

There are a few good "how to study" books on the market from which to choose. I realize that most students barely have time to read one how-to-study book, let alone try to compare and choose the best one. In this book, you will find practical, how-to suggestions that will help you—every day—to become a better student.

Achieve Excellence on Your Own Terms: How to Use This Book

Achieving Academic Excellence: How to Study can help you excel in your studies. This book is designed to give you the tools that will help you get the most out of your education. For some of you, reading this book will be the first time you have ever taken any extra steps in becoming a better student. Welcome to the world of academics. I hope your experiences here are rewarding and fulfilling. For others, this may be your third or fourth self-help book. The tips and techniques you learn here will assist you too.

Studying is serious work, and succeeding at your schoolwork is very important. There is a lot at stake for you as a student, whether you are a high school student who hopes to better your grades so you can get into a top college, or you are a college student who simply needs to bring up your grades. To achieve your goal, you need to learn the art of studying. This book can help.

Academic success at this stage in your life will give you a solid foundation for your future. All your future achievements, both in and out of the classroom, will have their roots in the education you receive today. I know it sounds corny, but think of today as the beginning of your future. What your future holds is largely up to you. It will be what you make it!

If you decide to "wait until later" to get serious about your studies, you run the risk of developing bad study habits now. Later, when you try to get serious about academics (and by the way, for most procrastinators, "later" never arrives), you will have many bad reading and study habits to unlearn—you will be working from a real deficit. You are fooling yourself if you think that procrastinating is a valid plan!

So how do you take hold of the future and start preparing for it today? Decide that the most important job that you have is being a student—and not just any student—but one that does his or her best at every turn. Your commitment to success and your dedication to becoming an academic star are worth more than all the words written in this or any other book about studying. You alone hold the key to your future.

Don't let your circumstances dictate what your future will be. Academics are one of the few areas of life where we all have a fairly level playing field. Granted, there are some whose station in life gives them access to the best schools and resources, but even those students must do the hard work of a student to succeed. Simply attending the best schools is no guarantee of success. It is still up to each individual student to do his or her best. Your commitment to success will be the thing that puts you over the top.

This book is designed to assist you once you have made the commitment to achieving your best. Achieving Academic Excellence: How to Study can be used as a step-by-step process that incorporates each chapter in succession. Each section also has its own merits. I understand that you may already employ certain habits and techniques that suit you and achieve satisfactory results for you. You may only need assistance with one area of your study regimen. If that is the case, Achieving Academic Excellence: How to Study can help you strengthen that area of weakness.

Having now given you license to utilize only parts of this book, I feel compelled to say that there are some points that I believe are essential to achieving your academic goals. The most important is the daily review of your class notes. Often, what separates the exceptional students from the merely good students is the consistent, conscientious review of class notes. Chapter Five, "Reviewing Your Notes and Study Skills," is a must read!

Even if you are interested in only one area of this book, I recommend that you read the entire book through once. You may find that you can take advantage of more of the material than you thought. The level of success you achieve is completely up to you. It's up to you to take responsibility for your academic career.

In Chapter Five, "Reviewing Your Notes and Study Skills," you will find a subsection titled "Use a Dictionary." Throughout this book, you will find words in **bold text.** These are words that may or may not be in your **vernacular** (or everyday language), and you may need to look them up in a dictionary. I did not include a glossary of terms in the back of the book. You need to become accustomed to using a dictionary, and there is no better time to begin than the present. I do not recommend one dictionary over another. The reference librarian at your school can give you a good recommendation on which dictionary is best for you.

The point of the bold text is twofold. First, to prod you into action. If you do not routinely use your dictionary to look up words with which you are unfamiliar, you are doing yourself a disservice. You should not go through life with the same vocabulary that you used when you were a child. Your vocabulary should always be growing. The bold text words have been chosen precisely to encourage readers to look up words in order to understand their full meaning.

Second, I am giving you an object lesson of what happens when you read a passage of text and you do not know the meaning of a word. You can stumble through and continue reading, but you will likely miss some intended meaning in the passage. You should use your dictionary to look up words, the meaning of which you do not know.

I suggest that with each bold text word that you look up, you note the word's meaning in the margin of the book. We remember more of what we write down than of what we only hear or read. The simple act of writing down the meaning will make you more likely to remember the word. Who knows, that word may become part of your everyday **vernacular.**

Happy Reading!

CHAPTER 1

Class Scheduling

The Master Plan
Required Classes
"Other" Classes
Professors
Geography
Master Plan Revisted

**"Where the heart is
the mind works best."**
Louisa May Alcott

S cheduling classes may seem like a strange place to begin the subject of how to study, but it is not. Deciding which classes to take is the first major decision you will make that will affect the rest of your semester. If this is your first semester in college, everything is new, exciting, and challenging. It is easy to let your enthusiasm guide you when choosing your first semester of classes. Don't do it. You need to choose your classes in a logical, well-calculated manner to maximize your time in college from your first day to your last. Don't overdo it. Pace yourself.

The Master Plan

To take full advantage of the classes that are offered, you must have a Master Plan for your education. Whether you are in a four-year university or a two-year trade school, you need a Master Plan. Your Master Plan must take into account the reason you are attending school. For example, if you have decided that you would eventually like to attend law

"Consider taking classes outside of your comfort zone."

school, you should consider the skills you will need to succeed in law school and schedule classes that move you toward that goal.

1

Using the example above, you would want to have several skills under your belt before you entered law school. You would want to be a good writer, a thorough reader, and a clear and confident public speaker. You may also want to explore some of the ethical dilemmas that an attorney might face. Your Master Plan would take all of this into consideration.

Likewise, if your goal is to own your own construction business, you will need to learn not only the hands-on skills of a carpenter and mason, but also the management and accounting skills it takes to run a business. If you were pursuing either of these careers and did not have the adequate foundation from these classes, your diploma would still look good in its frame on the wall. It just wouldn't be worth as much as it could have been worth if you'd had a Master Plan.

> "No one ever stopped to ask for directions when they had no destination. If you aren't headed anywhere, you don't need directions."

You need to be thinking about what you want to achieve with your education from the first day you schedule classes. Too many students float from one class to the next, one semester to the next, and end up with a hodgepodge of classes and an education that prepares them for very little. One of the chief complaints of employers is that new employees are not well prepared for the demands of the working world. You can put yourself ahead of the game by making a Master Plan before your first day of classes begins.

"But what if my plans change and I want to change my major?" you may ask. No problem. If you change your major, that signifies several things have happened. First, you have recognized that you were headed in the wrong direction. You may never have recognized that you were headed in the wrong direction if you hadn't made a plan and begun following it. A person who is driving and stops to get directions does so because he has not yet reached the destination and needs help in doing so. No one ever stopped to ask for directions when they had no destination. If you aren't headed anywhere, you don't need directions. Count yourself blessed if you see the need to change your major. It means that you have learned that you are not yet on the proper path and that you need to adjust your course.

Changing your major or shifting your educational focus shows that you are moving and progressing. You don't need to change directions if you are standing still. A preacher friend of mine told his parishioners that God could give direction to a moving vessel, but a vessel that was tied to the dock didn't need any direction. Changing your major is like that. You are moving—you simply need to move in another direction. Be smart. Use all the credits that you can. Try to take advantage of what you have already done to minimize any collateral damage. Also, remember that all learning has some redeeming value, even if the most important thing you learn is that you don't want to go in that direction any more.

If your first semester is prescribed for you, you should be thankful. Don't complain. I wish every school operated this way. The schools that prescribe a schedule for their first-year students understand that there is a lot to be gained from a regimented, predetermined schedule. This puts all the students on an even playing field. These schools also understand that they are relieving one more area of stress from a freshman's life by not making him or her choose a schedule. You will have at least three more years of scheduling classes, and by the end of your college career, you will look back fondly on the days when someone else made those decisions for you.

Required Classes

There are many required classes. These will cover basic educational requirements that I will refer to as one hundred level classes. You will also likely encounter basic educational requirements for your major. I will begin with the one hundred level classes.

The one hundred level classes may be taken at any time during your educational career. These classes are often thought of by new students as classes that must be gotten out of the way before taking "real" classes. You should not schedule these classes together, all in one or two semesters. Save some of them for later in your academic career. For example, if you need a one hundred level health class and two one hundred level physical education classes, there is a temptation to schedule one health class and one physical education class your first semester and your second physical education class your second semester to have these classes out of the way. I would not schedule them this way.

My recommendation is to save several of these classes for later in your third and fourth year when you need an easier class to relieve the pressure. These one hundred level classes are generally easier and require less time and effort than the more advanced classes. In the example above, I might schedule one of the three classes the first year, one the second year, and save one for either my third or fourth year. Later in your college career, you will be taking more demanding classes and will appreciate an easier, one hundred level class. Also, once you have two or three years of study under your belt, these classes will prove to be even easier for you. You will be able to get a good grade with less effort than if you had scheduled it your first semester.

Basic requirement classes in your major are a little different. These classes will be prerequisites for taking more advanced classes in your major. The absence of these classes could hold you back

4

later. You should look at the entire schedule of offerings for classes in your major from the first day you begin scheduling classes. Look at the advanced classes that you would like to take at some point in your academic career. Determine what the prerequisites are. You will see that several classes have prerequisites that overlap and some that have more than one prerequisite. There is nothing more disheartening than to learn that you cannot take the class that you want because you lack one of the prerequisites.

Remember, your goal is to get a great education. Scheduling classes is your first step in reaching that goal.

Having perused all the offerings in your major, determine which prerequisite classes will help you further your goals and try to schedule them first. These prerequisite classes will often fall within the required major basic classes. You can often begin to take them your first semester. If your school does not permit you to take these classes your first semester, then schedule these classes at your earliest opportunity. The point is to manage your class choices from the end to the beginning, and not the other way around. You should have a good idea of what classes you would like to take during your third and fourth year and then work toward that end by taking the appropriate classes that will get you there.

I understand that your goals may change and that you may decide to take a different direction in your education. Don't worry. By understanding the process of choosing your classes with a Master Plan, and thinking from the end to the beginning, you can always make the appropriate adjustments.

Other Classes

Another scheduling consideration is how many classes you should take outside your major. When you add up the one hundred level classes and the credits required for your major, you will find that you still have a few credits left to use anywhere you choose. There is a temptation to take these extra credits, usually called electives, within your major. Most students think, "Since I'm going to be a biologist, I should take every single biology class available." While I understand the thinking behind this statement, I want to suggest another strategy. I believe that it is in your best interest not only to strengthen your knowledge in your major, but also to broaden your general knowledge as well. You should take advantage of the fact that this is one time in your life when learning for learning's sake is an acceptable way to spend your time.

You should entertain the idea of taking classes that are outside of what you would routinely expect from yourself. This is what I mean: Anyone who knows me would likely tell you that I am an even-tempered person with generally conservative economic views and fairly conservative social views. You would not expect to find me in a Women Writers class, but that was one of the classes I scheduled during my undergraduate studies. I decided to take a Women Writers class from a well-known and often-published feminist. This class was a great opportunity to hear a new point of view. I was one of three males in a class of thirty and was challenged in many ways. Today, more than 20 years later, I am very glad that I took that class. It helped me to understand a different point of view.

Each of us has our own comfort zone. You should consider taking classes that are outside of your zone. Expand your horizons. Taking classes that challenge you to think in new ways or view things from a different point of view will be an investment, not only in your education, but also in being a well-rounded, functioning member of society.

Another reason to step outside your major when taking elective classes is to assist you in shoring up general areas of knowledge where you may be weak. For example, if you have never been able to balance your own checkbook, now is the time to take an Accounting 101 class to learn the basics of accounting. Perhaps you never learned to swim. Take swimming for non-swimmers. Most colleges and universities offer such classes.

To take advantage of classes that shore up your general life knowledge, do the following simple exercise. Write down on a piece of paper the six things you wish you could do or accomplish. You immediately thought of at least one or two, almost involuntarily. Make a list of the six things you would like to improve and keep it with this book (to help you remember where you put it). The next time you look at the availability of classes for an upcoming semester, take out this list and see if any of the offerings match your list. This is an easy way to begin, almost immediately, to make practical use of the offerings at your school.

Another reason to schedule elective classes outside of your major is for self-enrichment. While this is similar to the point above, it has a distinct difference. It is true that taking classes "outside of the box" will likely be enriching, but that is not the reason you are taking them. You schedule those classes to challenge yourself. Scheduling self-enrichment classes falls under the category of scheduling classes in your areas of interest. That is, if you were a windsurfer before you came to school, and there is a windsurfing class offered, take the course to further your preexisting interest.

Self-enriching classes can be the most fun classes. My undergraduate degree required two physical education classes. I scheduled golf as one of them. I liked to golf when I was in college, though I was not very good at it. It turned out that my golfing class required we pair up. My partner was the top quarterback at my university who went on to an NFL career! Take advantage of the classes that are offered if you have room in your schedule.

Professors

Next, when scheduling your classes, consider who will be teaching each class. During your early semesters, this may not be a great consideration, as there may be prescribed professors that you must schedule. If this is the case, don't waste any time fretting about it. There is no use worrying about what you have no power to change.

"The trivial round, the common task, Would furnish all we ought to ask."
John Keble

If it is in your power to take a certain class from professor A, B, or C, try to learn what you can about the professors before scheduling. Upperclassmen will be your best source on this issue. You should ask about the professor's attendance policy, grading scale and criteria, whether the professor gives quizzes, and how hard the finals are. These are questions that only a student who has studied with a specific professor can answer. Take the advice of several upperclassmen, when available, and come to your own conclusion. Don't mistake one student's bad experience with a true critique of a professor's teaching ability.

Professors are like all other professionals. Some are better than others, and some have maintained their passion for their particular subject, while others have only smoldering embers where flames once existed. There are many reasons for this. Tenure is one of them. Tenure can be a wonderful thing for professors, as it takes away the worries they have for their own future and permits them to concentrate on the subject matter they love. I have studied with many tenured professors who loved the subject they taught, and their enthusiasm was contagious and made the class come alive.

Tenure can also have a negative influence on a professor. Professors who are no longer interested in their subject matter or in working at being the best teacher or communicator they can be sometimes simply go through the motions, year after year. These professors know that there is little the college or university can do to discipline them because they are tenured. I have had classes with this type of professor also, and these classes can be dreadful.

Taking classes where a teaching assistant (TA) carries out much of the instruction is a roll of the dice. A TA is usually a graduate student who is pursuing an advanced degree. A typical TA has his or her own course load of classes, plus a class to teach on behalf of a tenured professor. Like everything else in life, the quality of instruction the TA provides depends on the character of the TA and the effort that he or she puts into the material.

If your TA can't wait to become a full-time professor one day and takes teaching very seriously, diligently preparing for every class, you may have a rewarding experience. If your TA looks at teaching your class as a "necessary evil," your class can turn into an endurance test. The "endurance test" classes are also part of your education. A diploma, a certificate of completion, a degree says, "I not only graduated and learned my craft, I learned how to put up with some inferior instruction and still came out ahead." When you find yourself in this kind of class, it is still up to you to make the most of it. You control the destiny of your education and what you gain from it.

Geography

Another consideration when scheduling your classes is geography. Find out where different classes are located in proximity to one another. I once scheduled twelve credits in an eight-week summer session. The workload was immense, and to add to the pressure, I unwittingly scheduled classes that were nearly one mile from each other on our very large campus. I had about fifteen minutes to get from one class to the other. When you must carry your books and related paraphernalia for an entire morning of classes, one mile can seem like ten!

If you are attending a small school, this may not be much of a consideration. Make sure you check on physical education classes, usually held at or near the school's gymnastic facilities, which might not be close to the main campus. Also check any "field study" classes, which may require you to go off-campus to complete the class.

Master Plan Revisited

Finally, when scheduling your classes, put together a Master Plan that includes at least your first two years of study, and preferably your entire college career, from **matriculation** to graduation. This may seem daunting, but it is well worth it. There are a few steps you need to take before you schedule your classes.

First, why are you in school? What is your goal? Some of you reading this may respond with "Gee, I'm not sure. I just want to get a good job after I graduate." Even if you answered in this way, you can still use this ambiguous answer to help you plan your college career. Let me use that "get a good job" answer as my example to show you what I mean.

If you want to get a good job when you graduate, what should you do today? First, you need to find out a few things, like where the good jobs are in the job market generally, and find out what the good jobs are in your geographic area. Where do you find this type of information?

I could list dozens of sources for you, but that would be spoon-feeding you the information. College professors will not treat you that way, so neither will I.

Go to your local library and ask a reference librarian for assistance with your research. Reference librarians can be your best resource. Once you have determined what the best jobs are, find two or three jobs that you feel you could be happy working in. You now have a goal to aim at. Will your goal change? Probably. But the next time you decide that you want to change direction, you will have some background to work with, and you will know where to get more information.

Also, when you say, "All I want is to get a good job," you are not being completely honest. If your research of the "good" jobs turns up several good-paying, secure jobs that you know would make you miserable and you summarily cross them off the list, you are, by process of elimination, choosing what you want to do with your life. Having to choose two or three jobs as goals at this early point in your college career will help give you some direction, even though those goals are likely to change.

Once you have identified your potential career choices, go to the related industry resources and learn all you can about that industry and that job. Try to determine what education is necessary to succeed in this industry. Does it require an advanced degree to really succeed? Does it require two years of overseas study? Are you willing to do what is necessary to succeed in this industry?

If you are a person of faith, pray. Ask God to help you choose. I believe God is always speaking. We, however, are not always listening.

Also, you need to determine what skills are necessary to succeed in this field. Is it math-intensive? Do you like math classes?

Is it heavy on written communication? Do you like writing? Can you handle taking writing-intensive classes to hone your writing skills? Determining what you need to succeed will assist you when it comes time to schedule your classes.

Try talking to someone you know who is already in the field that you are targeting. He or she will be able to give you advice on what classes you will need to take and what you need to know to succeed. Don't be afraid to ask for help. Most of us are flattered when a young person looks to us as an expert or a resource. You will get very few rejections at this stage.

The next step is creating your Master Plan. Use the information you have gathered and choose classes that will further your ultimate goal.

Perhaps you are thinking that all this talk about scheduling is too much micromanagement or that it is unnecessary. If you think you will just take what everybody else is taking or that you will worry about that when the time comes, you are in for an unpleasant surprise. With the considerable number of students vying for the same classes, it takes a good game plan and a commitment to carrying it out for your plan to succeed. Good planning now will pay great dividends later.

Self Assessment

To take advantage of classes that increase your general life knowledge, write down the six things you wish you could do or accomplish.

1.

2.

3.

4.

5.

6.

Now, make another list of six things in your life that you would like to improve.

1.

2.

3.

4.

5.

6.

When you next schedule classes, take out this list and see if any of the offerings match the items on your lists.

CHAPTER 2

In-Class Habits

Sit in the front of the room.
Attend class.
Introduce yourself to the professor
Ask and answer questions
Overcome obstacles to speaking in class

"Success or failure in business is caused more by the mental attitude even than by mental capacities."
Walter Scott

There is only one person who controls your destiny in each of your classes, and that is you. Don't be one of those students who, at the end of sixteen weeks of classes says, "If the professor's syllabus had been clearer I would have done better in this class," or "She never made herself very clear, and that is why I did poorly in her class." These students are merely pushing their responsibilities onto someone else. Take charge by setting the tone for a successful semester in each class. Here are several ways to assist you in taking charge and setting a positive tone that will carry you through your entire semester.

One of the most important in-class habits you need to master is note taking. This subject is so important that I have devoted an entire chapter to it. I will leave this and move on to other, in-class habits, but the reader should understand that I deem note taking a critical skill that must be mastered in order to succeed in your studies.

Attend Class

First, attend class. Remember that you miss class at your own peril. Attending class will help you know what the professor deems the most important part of the material.You will sometimes hear

14

students say, "You don't need to attend his class. He tests directly from the book." Even if it is one hundred percent accurate that he tests from the book, you should still attend class. The professor will cover the material from the text that he or she thinks is the most important. If it is straight from the book, so be it. You at least have the advantage of knowing what the professor covered in class. And the professor will give you clues as to what he or she thinks is the most important point of the text. You won't be able to catch those clues, however, if you are not in class.

How does a professor give clues as to what is important in a text? When he or she gives an example that deviates from the examples given in the text, you know you are in an area that the professor deems important—so important that he or she came up with new examples to emphasize the point. You can bet that it will make its way onto the test.

Also, by attending every class, you are saying to the professor, "I think your class is important and interesting." You are sending a signal, however subtle, that this class is important to you too. You are **ingratiating** yourself to the professor by simply attending his or her class. When you pay tuition, you are paying for the opportunity to learn from scholars who specialize in particular fields of study. It only makes sense to take advantage of all the instruction for which you are paying. You are not simply buying a degree—you are investing in yourself by investing in an education.

Perhaps you attend a school that has a mandatory attendance rule. If so, you are in the minority. Count it a blessing. You are being forced to benefit from this tip.

Even if your school has no mandatory attendance rule, you are still not in the clear from being penalized for not attending class. A friend of mine who teaches at a highly respected school of music created a very inventive way of getting around the lack of a mandatory attendance rule at the university where he teaches. He gives an in-class oral quiz whenever the whim strikes him, and the whim usually strikes him on a day of low attendance. For his oral quiz, he reads each student's name aloud and asking a simple question about the material assigned for that day. He asks the first student—who happens to be present—and she answers correctly, giving her a one hundred percent on the quiz. He calls the next name—who happens to be absent—reads the question aloud again, and that student receives a zero on the quiz. Thus, attending the class is beneficial when it comes to the final grade.

Sit in the Front of the Room

Sitting in the front of the room cuts out all the distractions that occur behind you. I know that this sounds too simple, but don't discount it for that reason. How many times have you been sitting in a class and been distracted by the class clown or by students passing notes? Sitting in front of the room cuts out these needless distractions.

By sitting in the front of the room, you are also making a conscious decision to attend the class, as the professor is more likely to notice when you are missing, even if he or she does not have a mandatory attendance rule. You thus put pressure on yourself to attend every class, and this is the right kind of pressure—pressure to achieve your best.

You may be thinking, "That's fine for some, but not for me. I want to remain anonymous," or "I'm too shy to do that." Don't allow your excuses, your fears, or your "legitimate reasons" keep you from becoming the best student possible. Only a conscious decision from you will move you in the right direction. Challenge yourself to overcome your obstacles.

Another reason to sit in the front of the class is to help you pay attention. Sitting in the front of the room forces you to listen and to watch what is happening in front of you. You cannot hide from the professor! It is also difficult to allow yourself to daydream when the professor is only a few feet away.

A personal anecdote on paying attention: I once had a class in which I found it difficult to pay attention because of the professor's monotone voice. The material was interesting and the professor was extremely well read, but the delivery was very dry. I found myself dozing off (the class began at 8:00 AM and lasted until late morning), and my mind wandered. I came up with a unique solution.

I would stop by the convenience store each morning and purchase a medium-sized pink grapefruit juice. This was my salvation. You see, I hate the pungent taste of grapefruit juice. Just thinking about it makes my mouth pucker! I kept the cap on the juice for the first forty-five minutes because I could

> *"You must make the decision that you are going to succeed."*

stay with the professor that long. I uncapped the juice after forty-five minutes and took a sip every five to ten minutes (my own version of nursing a drink). It kept me awake and alert enough to stay with the professor. I ended up at the top of the class.

Do whatever it takes to succeed. Remember my "grapefruit juice" example, and create your own success stories!

A final word of encouragement about sitting in front of the room: please don't hide behind "I'm an introvert" thinking. Whether you are an outgoing gregarious sort of person or a true introvert, you will benefit from being at the front of the room and paying attention. It does not mean that you have to be someone you are not. Just remind yourself that the reason you are in school is to learn and to get the most out of your education. You can overcome almost anything if your goal is clear enough.

Introduce Yourself to the Professor

Next, introduce yourself to the professor. Even if you are in a one hundred level class with hundreds of students, take the time to politely introduce yourself. This immediately distinguishes you from the nameless faces and the faceless numbers. Professors are people too, and most would prefer to know that their efforts are for the benefit of a person, not a number. Many professors know that due to the size of the class or the total class-load that they carry, they will only get to know a handful of students. Be one of that handful. I suggest you choose the first or second day of class for making this introduction.

After your initial introduction, wait a week or so and then create some reason to speak to the professor again. You could ask a question concerning the day's lecture or a homework assignment. By communicating with your professor again, just a short time after your first encounter, you reinforce who you are. You are putting a name with the face for them and this is crucial. It could pay big dividends later in the semester to have them know you as a person. If they are on the fence some time later in the semester concerning your grade, you will more likely be given the benefit of the doubt if they know you as a person.

Ask and Answer Questions

Next, ask questions. Answer questions. I know this one also sounds simple, but it is a terribly underutilized in-class technique. If you are in a class that bores you so thoroughly that you are never prompted, even once, to ask a question or become involved in a class discussion, ask yourself why you are in that class.

Asking questions serves several purposes. First, it is important to be honest with yourself and your professor. Professors routinely ask, "Does anyone have any questions?" You need to be honest. If you still do not understand something a professor has explained or gone over, you should raise your hand and tell the professor. And if you don't understand, you can rest assured that someone else in your class also doesn't understand. Asking your question may serve to educate the entire class.

Second, asking questions in class helps keep you interested. There are times when class work and lectures can get to be a grind. You are asking a lot of yourself to sit through a full load of classes week after week, and it's only natural for you to occasionally grow weary. When you feel yourself slipping into a blasé attitude about a class, you need to force yourself to pay attention. One good trick is to force yourself to formulate a question about what the professor is covering at that moment. This forces you to focus on the subject matter at hand.

Third, asking questions will separate you from the silent members of the class. Your goal should be to do the best you can and learn all you can while you are studying. By asking questions, you put yourself on the professor's map. The professor knows who you are, at least for that moment, and will address your question and work to educate you. Those who sit silently will not have this opportunity for individualized instruction or assistance.

Overcome Obstacles to Speaking in Class

Many students feel too intimidated by their professors to ask questions. Others fear what their peers may think of them. Whatever name you give this obstacle, it is fear, and fear has a way of robbing us of many of life's most wonderful experiences. Whatever your reason for being slow to speak in class, I want to give you just one way to help you overcome this obstacle. There are many other viable techniques to deal with fear of public speaking. Perhaps you can schedule a Public Speaking class if you care to learn more about this subject.

If you are stricken at the thought of speaking in class, you need to ask yourself why you are in school. This strikes directly at the root of the problem. Why are you in school? Is it to learn engineering? Music? Are you in school to get a good job when you graduate? Whatever your reason, the answer to this question will help you get past your fear of speaking in class.

"You have to see every class on your schedule, every lecture of every class, as a small part of the entire package that you need to succeed."

Let's use the example of engineering. You are in school to become an engineer and you are in an entry-level engineering class. The professor is explaining a concept that is foreign to you. You are sitting in class and feeling as if you are the stupidest person there because you are the only one who is lost and does not get what the professor is explaining. If you fail to ask a question now, when you need to have the point clarified, you will continue into the semester with a damaged foundation of knowledge. You may understand many of the other concepts taught later in the semester, but they are all based, at least in part, on your faulty knowledge. Your damaged foundation is no better than a house with a wonderful living room and kitchen and three beautifully finished bedrooms all built on a faulty foundation. A house with a faulty foundation is doomed! So is your knowledge in this class.

If you say that the reason you are in school is to become an engineer, then that means you should understand everything about engineering to the best of your ability. By permitting a point to get by you without making every effort to understand it, you are saying that you do not really care if you know everything you need to know to become an engineer. It also is a passive way of showing that you don't really care if you reach your goal of becoming an engineer. I know those both sound extreme, but they are true. Do you care more about the need to feel protected by not speaking up than the need to learn this new material? Would you rather sit silently and not reach your goal or risk it and push forward toward your goal?

You should see every class on your schedule, every lecture of every class, as a small part of the entire package that you need to succeed. It is easy to justify to yourself that "It won't matter if I miss this one little point . . . I'll catch it later in the semester." Sadly, as the semester passes, this may not be the case.You will likely be more accustomed to your fear of asking questions, making it easier for you to say something like, "I have a basic understanding of this point. I'm sure I can pull a B on the test." By not setting your standard high every day, you lower the overall standard of what you are willing to settle for.

Don't ever settle for less than your best. Both fear and apathy are terrible things. You owe it to yourself to give one hundred percent to your academic endeavors. You don't want to look back on your college experience with regret. Always aim high.

Are you in school to become an engineer? Then ask the questions that you need to ask, or answer the question that no one else attempts to answer. Remember that you picked up this book to become a better student. Take the initiative. What was the first sentence in this chapter? Go back and re-read it if you don't remember. Remembering the **vignette** about the engineering student should help you remember to not build a faulty knowledge foundation of your own. Speak up in class.

Self Assessment

To become a better student, I need to improve my in-class habits by . . .

1.

2.

3.

4.

5.

6.

When you begin your next semester of classes, take out this list to remind yourself of the areas in which you want to improve.

CHAPTER 3

Working with Your Professors

Personalities
Learn the Professor's rules
and stay within them

"... One of the greatest problems of our time is that many are schooled but few are educated."
Thomas Moore

We don't all get along. There is no magic pill that will make you like some people or make them like you. That's just human nature. We must, however, be able to function civilly with everyone with whom we have any social contact. It is imperative that you learn to interact positively with your professors. Getting along with a professor with whom you have nothing in common or for whom you feel nothing but **antipathy** falls into the category of functioning civilly.

You will, undoubtedly, have a class in your college career with an "unlikable" professor. There can be any number of reasons for the discord you feel with the professor. Don't waste your time trying to get to the root of the problem. Instead, find a way to function in his or her class without your personal feelings getting in the way. This is sometimes easier said than done. Here are a few helpful hints.

Personalities

First, remember why you are in school. It is not to befriend every one of your professors. It is to learn. You have a goal and a vision for your college career. Keep your eyes focused on your goal. Each professor has a part to play in your education.

Next, bear in mind that your professor has had hundreds or even thousands of students come through his or her classes before you and will likely have that many more after you are gone. Do you think your professor has gotten along with every one of the students he or she has taught? Of course not. I'm sure that most could tell you stories of students with whom they had great difficulty during their tenure as a professor. Did your professor allow that to stop him? No. Why not? Because teaching is the professor's job. The idea of being stymied by a poor relationship between the student and the professor would raise a laugh from most professors. They would tell you the reason they plow through when personality problems arise is that it is their responsibility to teach—learning is the student's responsibility.

Don't allow the fact that you do not like a professor stop you from learning. Decide that you are going to learn all that you possibly can from each professor. You have made a commitment to yourself to do your best. Allowing a personality conflict to slow down your learning is nothing more than an excuse for not working hard in that class. Don't allow anything to become an excuse for not achieving your very best in school.

> "Try to find a way to interact positively with your professors."

Once you have gotten past the excuse of a personality conflict, take the next step. Try to find a way to interact positively with your professor. In most instances this is not too difficult, as professors are

24

usually delighted to work with students who are eager to learn.

If have you tried motivating yourself to remember why you are in school, and you have tried to get in step with the professor, but you still are not able to follow his or her teaching, I suggest going directly to the source. Speak to the professor and be kind, but direct. Always be diplomatic in everything you say.

For example, if you have tried to follow a professor's class lecture in every way you can, but you still can't come up with the right mix of enthusiasm and understanding to get through the class, go to the professor and ask for help. Do not, however, start by saying something like "I just don't get you, man!" Perhaps a gentler approach, such as, "I'm not sure I have grasped all that I should from today's class," will yield a better response. Always put the onus on yourself. Your professors will be more likely to reach out their hands to assist you if you say to them "I am failing to do something right, please help me."

I had a few classes where I had a very difficult time aligning myself with what the professor expected of me. In those instances, I tried to find that middle ground by diplomatically approaching the professor as stated above. This is your best bet to making the most out of a class with what I call an "unlikable" professor.

If you have read the "In-Class Habits" chapter, you already know several ways of interacting with your professors. Don't hesitate to speak in class, ask questions, or volunteer information. Also, remember that class attendance counts for a lot with most professors.

Learn the Professor's Rules and Stay Within Them

Having a leader is important for every endeavor in life. Whether it's playing a pick-up baseball game, running a small business, flying a jetliner, or running a university, a leader is needed in every situation.

Your classes are no different. Your professor is your leader. It's up to you to follow.

Learn each professor's style of leading. Some are strict totalitarians who expect rigid obedience. Others are "do-your-own-thing" professors who allow for a more relaxed classroom experience. Learn what each professor expects and stay within those limits. Don't try to impose your idea of how a class should be run. You can do that when you become a professor. For now, fall in line with your professor's expectations. Your experience with that professor will be much more enjoyable for both of you.

Just as every endeavor has a leader, every leader has a rhythm or cadence they expect you to march to. Try to understand what each professor expects in class and on homework assignments. If you can get in step with your professor by understanding what he or she expects, then you will have a better chance of succeeding in that class.

Finally, remember that (just like you) professors can have bad days too. Don't hold your professors to stratospheric standards of excellence or conduct. Give them the same breaks you allow yourself. Most professors enjoy teaching and love their subject matter. Try to tap into their joy in teaching their subject. You may discover you can march to their cadence after all.

Self Assessment

To help you learn to work with your professors, take a moment and recall a time when you had to work with someone in authority to continue your progress. It may have been a time when you had to compromise with a teacher in grade school, a scout master who was overbearing on your merit badges, or even a time when you had to work with your parents (arrgghh!) to buy that great new car you wanted!

Now, use the above example to motivate you the next time you confront a situation where you must work within your professor's rules, no matter how ridiculous you think they are. Remind yourself that, "If I was able to do this, I can surely work with my professor."

CHAPTER 4

Note Taking

Do Take Notes.
The type of notebook you choose
Other considerations
What do I write down?
Paraphrasing
The blank left page
What do I write down?

**"One's work may be
finished someday, but
one's education never."**
Alexandre Dumas

Few things have the potential to assist your quest for learning and doing your best in school as much as good note taking skills. The notes you take in class, along with the other materials I suggest you put in your notebook, will become the foundation of your study materials for each of your classes.

There are several books devoted to nothing but note taking. I will not try to give you a treatise approach to this subject but will relay to you only what I believe you will need to know about taking notes and getting the most out of your education, including better grades.

Psychologists tell us that we remember eight times more of the things we write down than those that we simply hear. That is an amazing statistic! Think about the ramifications of writing down simple tables or theorems. Most of us can remember the full text of lengthy materials, such as the Star-Spangled Banner, by rote memory alone. Imagine how much more you could learn by writing it down.

Do Take Notes

First and most important, TAKE NOTES in every one of your classes. You may not be accustomed to taking notes and this may feel awkward— "What should I write down? What if I'm the only one writing anything down?" Stay calm. These are common questions and we'll address each of your concerns.

First, remember that you will not see peer pressure on your grade report at the end of the semester . . . you will only see your final grade. You must learn to withstand thoughts of "what will the others think." Remember, the reason you are in school is to learn. If this way of looking at peer pressure is new for you, so be it. The sooner you learn to deal with the peer pressure, the better off you will be.

I am not suggesting you go out and purchase a pocket protector and become a full-fledged nerd. I'm only suggesting that college is a time for you to begin to form your own personality and identity. You are reading this book—whether you purchased it or it was given to you as a gift—because you decided that you want to be a better student. If this is true, then decide now (because only a decision from you will make it happen) that you are willing to do what it takes to be a good student and achieve your goals, even if that means you are the only one in class taking notes. I've been that student—you will live to talk about it! If you have a class in which taking notes is not required because of the special nature of the class or because the materials handed out by the professor thoroughly cover the material, fine. You will learn in time whether you can forego taking notes in a particular class. In the meantime, assume that you need to take notes in every class in order to succeed.

Remember, the very act of writing down information—as opposed to only hearing it or reading it—helps solidify the information in your own mind. Make a quality decision to take notes.

The Type of Notebook You Choose

Next, before we address the what and how of note taking, let's talk about where you are going to take notes. There are a multitude of notebooks and note-taking systems commercially available for students today. Don't get suckered into purchasing a slick, five-part, three-step note-taking system. While these products may look good, if you are a person who has never used such a complex system before, you will not likely be comfortable using one at this point. Habits must change first; the accoutrements can come later. Become a better note taker and student first, and add the slick notebook system later.

I recommend using one small three-ring binder for each class. You may be able to put more than one subject in a larger notebook, but I don't recommend it. I only spent a few dollars for a half dozen three-ring binders, and I used those same binders throughout my entire undergraduate career. You don't need to invest a fortune.

Using a three-ring binder allows you to add and remove pages and to insert additional information or remove certain pages for studying or copying. In addition to in-class notes, it is very helpful to insert returned quizzes and tests into your three-ring binder. (Such papers are wonderful study guides, but more on that subject later.) It is also useful to insert any handouts from the professor directly into your notebook. In this way, you are creating one location for all your important materials for each class.

Some students may prefer using an individual spiral-bound notebook for several classes. This does not work as well, for the reasons stated above. You cannot add information that you may have missed and removing pages becomes messy very quickly.

Other Considerations

You should have a permanent home for your notebooks, no matter what note-taking system you use. Choose a place in your room that you know is safe and accessible. You want to be able to get to your notebooks quickly on those mornings that you awaken with just enough time to dash to class.

Choose whether you will use a pen or a pencil to take notes. Some say you should always use a pencil when taking notes to make it easier to change them later, should you need to do so. It is easy to make a mistake when furiously taking down a professor's long or detailed statement. Using a pencil does make it easier to make changes. Pencil, on the other hand, smears more easily than pen, and smeared notes may be difficult to read when studying.

Pens make a clearer mark, making your notes easier to study from later. Your class notes—the basic building block of your study materials throughout the semester—will be easier to mark up and highlight if they are in pen. I usually used a blue ink pen for my note taking and a yellow highlighter and red felt-tip marker to mark up my notes when studying. A highlighter will smear pencil marks and eventually make the highlighter unusable. You will have to choose what works best for you. Either way, stick with your decision for at least one semester. You can always re-evaluate it at the end of the semester.

What Do I Write Down?

This is what ninety percent of your classmates are also thinking, so don't be alarmed. Most of you are in the same boat. My suggestions will make you a better note taker, which will, in turn, give you better information from which to study. Remember that you are building the foundation of your study materials when you are taking notes. Each day you take accurate notes, you are building a stronger and stronger foundation for yourself.

As to what you will need to write down in your notes, let me first address a few things you should not do.

Call these the "don'ts" of note taking:

1. Don't try to take down every word the professor utters. I have seen this backfire many, many times. By taking down every

word, students feel that they are capturing the knowledge that the professor is relaying. In truth, writing down virtually every word only proves how good someone is at transcribing. You could record the lecture if that was what you wanted to do.

2. Don't worry if you do not catch every detail of a phrase or a summary the professor was giving. Write down all you can, and then fill in the missing portions later. You will be able to ask a classmate for the missing elements of the equation, or you may have to speak to the professor to fill in your missing data. Either way, the missing information is available. If you allow missing something to upset or unnerve you, you will miss even more of what follows. Just keep going and resolve to get the missing material after class.

3. Don't be so tied to your note taking that you cannot put down your pen and join the discussion. Your professor is being paid to share his or her knowledge with you. Taking notes should not keep you from getting involved in the class. Even if you need to go back and fill in your notes after class, stay involved in the class discussion. Here is an example, from a non-educational setting, of how being too involved in recording events can cause you to miss them:

> I once visited the Gettysburg battlefield with my family and saw a man with a video camcorder recording every inch of the history in front of him. His wife said to him, "Put that thing down and look at this." He replied, "I'm getting it all on tape. I'll look at it tonight when we get home." This man will not get to experience the battlefield the same way he could have, had he simply put down his camcorder and looked around for himself.

4. Don't worry about what the others in your class are doing regarding note taking. Take care of yourself. After your class has progressed long enough for you to identify the top students, you may want to

talk to those students and compare notes from class. You may be able to learn a great deal from top students' notes.

Here are some of the "dos" of note taking:

1. Try to focus on what the professor deems important. This is actually much easier than it sounds. Consider the following:

> If you had to teach a class about something—let's say cooking a spaghetti dinner—how would you begin? You would first cover the basics, like the necessary ingredients, the proper utensils, etc. Whether your style is to then go into great detail or to just give a basic outline, you would follow some logical course from the beginning with your raw ingredients all the way to the end when you are serving a steaming plate of spaghetti.

Your professor is going to do the same thing with almost every class and semester he or she teaches. The professor knows what basic information is necessary for you to understand the material that is to follow. He or she will begin with the "raw ingredients" that you need to understand and will then, and only then, proceed with the remainder of the lecture or class.

The "raw ingredients" that the professor teaches you might take up the first five minutes of each class period, or perhaps the first three classes of the semester will be devoted to the "raw ingredients."It is up to you to locate those "raw ingredients" and be sure to take them down in your notes.

When trying to discern these raw ingredients, remember that your professors are people just like you. They organize things in a way that works for them. Keep this in mind each time you sit down in class. With just a little practice you will be able to discern when the professor is covering the "raw ingredients" and when he or she is covering the "cooking instructions." Do your best to get in step with each of your professors.

As you get more accustomed to discerning how the material your professor is covering fits into the bigger picture, you will more easily understand when you must be taking notes and when you can relax a little. I once had an algebra teacher who was a very clever storyteller. He would weave his subject matter in an out of his stories, so much so that it was sometimes hard to tell if he was trying to make a point about algebra or if he was speaking **tangentially**. The class finally learned that when his stories turned to fishing, he was on a tangent and we could put down our pencils! You will learn the same tips about your professors.

One final point in trying to assess what is important: remember that your professors were once students. They know exactly how it feels to sit in a class and wonder what is coming next. Most professors are going to make an attempt to make the subject matter understandable. They want you to succeed, they really do (at least most of them do). Don't look for hidden agendas, as in, "I'll bet she is just giving us this information to throw us off! She'll never put this on the test." Most professors have too much to cover in one semester. They don't have time for such childish games. The material that your professors present will likely be organized in some logical manner. It's up to you to try to follow their organization, keeping in mind that the most important "raw ingredients" will be given early on.

2. Take your notes in outline form.

This one takes some practice to master, but will yield incredible results during your entire academic career. The premise is the same as the previous—your professor is likely working from either a formal or an informal outline. You need to tap in to his or her thinking as much as possible. Try to produce an outline that closely mirrors the professor's own notes.

If there is an outline behind what is being taught, then shouldn't you use an outline to take it all down? Wouldn't it be great if you had the professor's notes to study from? It only makes sense. Here is a trick that will help you learn to take notes in outline form and also will help you follow where you are in the professor's outline during a class lecture.

Remember when you learned to write essays or paragraphs? You were taught that you needed a main point or thesis, at least three supporting facts, and a conclusion. Today, when you read a well-drafted paragraph or short article, you can usually separate the main point and the supporting facts fairly easily. The main point is usually at the beginning, and the supporting facts follow.

We are going to employ what you already know about paragraph construction to help you learn to take notes in outline form. Read the paragraph below, or even better, have someone read it aloud to you. As you read it or listen to it, write down the following:

A. The main point
B. The first supporting fact
C. The second supporting fact
D. The third supporting fact

Taking notes in outline form is not as difficult as you might think. Even if you are not a naturally organized person, you can still learn to be organized in your note taking. If you know the topic of a lecture, or can discover the topic by careful listening, you have your first heading. The information that describes or explains your topic will be the points below your heading.

Your outline for the paragraph above should look something like this:

> 1. Taking Notes—Outline Form
>   a.) Organization
>   b.) Find topic (heading)
>   c.) Support topic (subheadings)

This is not that difficult, though it is not automatic. It takes a little practice and patience. I recommend that you have someone read to you from a good newspaper like the Wall Street Journal. Choose any story and repeat the exercise above. You need to get into the practice of outlining what you hear. This skill will help you no matter what endeavor you choose as your life's work. I find it invaluable today in business and the practice of law. You will notice that it becomes easier with practice.

Once you have practiced this exercise a few times you will see that picking out the main point from the supporting facts is not difficult. You simply need to be a good, attentive listener and a quick **scrivener**.

One of my first college professors would start nearly every class with a rough outline of what she was going to cover. God bless her! Be sure to thank any professor who does the same for you. It was my object lesson in taking notes in outline form. After the professor put the outline on the board, we could follow where we were in her outline during the lecture, and we would know where we were headed.

As your class progresses, try to pick out the main points, which become headings in your outline, and to pick out the headings' supporting facts, which would come underneath those headings in your outline. Remember your practice sessions picking out the main topic from the supporting facts, and how it became easier with time. The same thing will happen with each class and each professor. It will simply take some practice.

In most classes, you walk into the room with at least a general idea of what subject or topic is being covered that day. If you had a reading assignment for that day, you know even more of what the professor is likely to cover. You can begin to sketch in your mind what that day's lecture is likely to look like in outline form. DON'T WRITE IT DOWN YET! You never know for sure what is coming, and you don't want to put the wrong things in your class notes. But you at least have an edge when that blank piece of paper is staring at you. Use all of this to your advantage to create class notes that are organized in an outline that will make mastering the material and studying for the next test even easier.

> *"Work from the assumption that your professor is using an outline."*

If you go into a class without a clue about what will be discussed that day, ask the professor to tell you what he or she expects to cover before class begins. Some professors will tell you that you just have to wait until class begins, but others will be only too happy to tell you.

The form of your outline should be simple. As you will learn in the blank left page section, you will have time to **interlineate** additional material later. Take down the main topics as headings. For example, if the topic is taking care of your mental health with exercise, I might start with "EXERCISE" as my first heading, and then listen to where the professor goes from there. If he begins talking about the various types of exercise available, I might put "TYPES" as my first subheading. If he instead begins talking about the physiological benefits of exercise, I might put down "BENEFITS" as a subheading and begin listing the benefits underneath, one by one. The point is to organize the material, as neatly as possible, in a logical manner, so that when you go back and read the notes, they are not just line after line of raw material. That last point is worth revisiting. *Without an outline, your notes will be little more than line after line of raw material.*

Don't worry if you can't seem to get the outline just right. Do your best. The very act of trying to put the information in some order is an act of synthesis, which will assist you in learning the material. Synthesizing material, instead of just spitting it back out the way you learned it, means that you have taken it in and are making it your own. You will master the art of taking notes in outline form with a little determination and practice.

If it seems that you cannot get in sync with the professor, no matter how hard you try, JUST KEEP GOING. I have two reasons for advising this. First, your outline is probably not as far off as you feel it is, and it may only need minor adjustments and not a complete reworking. Second, the very act of practicing will make you a better outliner and listener for the next class.

Reread this section, take your notes in outline form, as many times as necessary to grasp the fundamentals. Practice the Wall Street Journal exercise again. You can do it!

3. Be Sure You Get the Supporting Information, "Not Just the Raw Ingredients." You are creating an outline while your professor leads your class, and you are getting the most important "raw ingredients." Now you need to focus on the supporting information to properly fill in your outline.

The temptation in taking notes in outline form is to learn to pick out the most essential information, and allow the rest to go by the wayside. Don't get me wrong, no one sets out to make this mistake. You don't wake up and say, "Today I think I will really shoot myself in the foot and take really crappy notes!" It happens much more subtly. Perhaps like this . . .

> *You head for class knowing that your assigned reading for the day was about the influence of eastern religions in the United State in the twentieth century. You read the assignment, though perhaps not as thoroughly as you should have. You comfort yourself with the thought that the professor will cover the same material in class, and you decided last night when you were reading that you would not worry about getting bogged down in the details in your first reading.*

> *Your class begins and, having mastered the art of taking notes in outline form, you write down "EASTERN RELIGIONS—US—20th CENTURY" as your heading when the professor begins reviewing the assigned reading. As the lecture continues and begins to get into the meat of the presentation, you have a decision to make. Many students will stop short of taking accurate notes with the excuse "this information is all in the book . . . I can get it from there," or some similar **pabulum**.*

Don't be lazy! You knew that the information was in your textbook when you didn't take it seriously the night before! It would be so easy to let it pass by in class because you know you can always read it later from the textbook. This may seem to be a silly example, but ask students who have been through college if this has ever happened to them, and they will tell you that it has. Don't be as lazy about note taking today as you were the night before when reading.

Laziness and procrastination are two foes that confront the new

MARK A. MATEYA, ESQ.

college student every day. Their consequences can be devastating! Don't let them win! Control your own destiny, one class at a time, one day at a time, one semester at a time. Take good notes. Use the outline format.

I chose this area, taking notes on the supporting facts to talk about combating procrastination, because this is the area where procrastination will most likely raise its head first and most often. You will be tempted not to take thorough notes on supporting information because 1) it's in the book already; 2) no one else is writing anything down; 3) you don't want to appear too geeky; 4) and the list goes on and on.

> "Laziness and procrastination are two foes that confront the new college student every day."

These seem to be perfectly good justifications for not writing this material down. It is in your textbook, for goodness sake. If you think there is nothing more to getting an education and a college degree than simply possessing the knowledge in a book, I can save you lots of time and money. Get your class schedule for your entire four- or five-year curriculum, go to the college bookstore and buy all the books you will need, and then walk directly to the podium to collect your degree. You "possess" all the knowledge you need, right? I mean, it's in the book, right? Somehow, I doubt that your diploma will be waiting there for you. If this sounds silly to you now, remember it the next time you are tempted to skip taking good notes on supporting facts in class because you possess that information in a book. You must own it—make it your own.

If your professor thinks enough of a topic to talk about it in class, you need to put it in your class notes. Remember, you are getting the chance to study almost directly from the professor's own notes if you learn to take good, outlined notes in class. To do so requires that you take down all the supporting facts, not just the main topics.

4. Learn This Technique for Transcribing Long Passages
   There are times when you know that you need to get what the professor is saying verbatim, but you simply can't write that fast. Here is a good trick for you. Of course, if you already know shorthand, you do not need the simple advice I have to offer. If, however, you find yourself in class trying to write like the wind in longhand, this tip will help.

   Start by getting the first three or four words of the phrase exactly as stated. Next, take down the first letter (or two) of each word of the rest of the phrase, leaving enough space to fill in the word later. When the professor has completed the phrase, go back and immediately try to fill in the words from the letters you have transcribed. You will be surprised at how easily long passages can be transcribed in this way.

   Have someone read the following passage aloud to you. Practice the technique, taking down the first few words and the first letter of the following words.

   Assumption of the risk can best be described as an affirmative defense to negligence. It must be pled by the person against whom negligence is claimed.

   By taking down the beginning full words of the phrase, you give yourself an anchor. Often, hearing the beginning of the phrase will jog your memory enough to be able to repeat the entire phrase. The first letter of each of the remaining words will be additional clues to assist you in completing the phrase.

Repeat this exercise as often as necessary, using any material at hand. This technique is fairly easy to master.

You may find that by using this technique you have been able to retrieve seventy or eighty percent of the phrase, but not every word. If this is the case, before you start berating yourself for not having hit "record" on your smart phone, consider what you do have. You have most of the important information you need as it fits into your outline (which happens to mirror your professor's outline). You can now easily go to the professor or a respected student and ask for the missing word or two. It is not as if you are asking for the professor to teach the entire class over again. It is only a single phrase within the context of your classwork that you lack. Your basic knowledge is sound—you simply need assistance with one little piece of the puzzle.

5. Tips on how to write in your notes.

Finally, the answer to the million-dollar question, "What exactly do I write in my class notes?" If you have read the previous four tips, you know most of the answer to this question. The answer is quite simple: you take down in your notes whatever is dished out. I have simply given you some pointers on how and how much to write. Below is a helpful review of how your notes should look as well as a practical tip on what exactly you should write in your notes.

First, write as neatly as you can without sacrificing speed. You must be able to read the notes later for them to be worth anything to you.

Precisely what information you need to put in your class notes is divided, as previously stated, into vital information that is in the form of a heading and then the information that supports it follows. You put all this information into your notes in an understandable form, such that you can recall it later when you are reviewing your notes. And of course, all this information is taken down in outline form. It sounds like a lot, but taken one step at a time, it is not that difficult.

Don't try to get too wordy in your notes. You will be able to go back and interlineate with more exact information later. You want to write each idea clearly enough so that a later reading of your notes will bring back to you all you need to recall about the subject.

Also, if you need to have a section verbatim, such as a quote or a theorem, you should get it down using tip number four above.

So, let's suppose you are sitting in a lecture for the first time. What, if anything, do you write in your notes? First, if you had a reading assignment, you have a fair idea of what will be discussed in class. You want your notes to be logically ordered to follow the class discussion, and you can anticipate that the class discussion will likely follow the assigned reading. Therefore, you write down those things that relate to the reading and that the professor thought was important enough to mention in class. I know this seems very fundamental, but taking good notes is not rocket science. It follows a logical pattern.

Sometimes a professor will take a moment to write something on the board. This is a HUGE clue for you! Why would he or she write it down if it weren't important? You had better include it in your notes.

Another clue is when your professor refers directly to something that is in the text. This means the professor thinks the point is so important that he or she wants it to come to your attention three times. First when it was given as a reading assignment, second when it was referred to in class, and third when you review it in your own study time. The assigned readings are one of your biggest indicators as to what should be in your class notes.

43

What if there are no assigned readings or if the readings are always supplemental to the lecture? Then what do you do? You should listen carefully and try to pick up clues from other sources. Textbooks are usually only part of any class. Be as creative as you need to be in taking notes and being prepared for class. There is almost always some material, in some medium, that you must digest before class. Don't worry. If you are paying attention to what the professor tells you, even if it is "Be sure to watch the Discovery Channel at 8 PM tomorrow night," you will be prepared to take good class notes.

Taking good notes requires your effort and discipline, just like most everything else in your education. One of the benefits of learning to take good notes is that you will become a better listener and communicator in your daily life. Communication skills are not only verbal—they are auditory also. You must be a good listener, no matter what field you ultimately choose to go into. Good note taking skills will assist you throughout your entire career.

Finally, what do you do if you do not have any idea what material will be covered in class? Remember that we decided that essential information in a lecture is like the "basic ingredients" of a recipe. Listen for this "basic ingredient" information and be sure you take good notes on it. Next you will listen for the "cooking instructions" that explain how to use those basic ingredients, all the while taking notes in outline form that will enable you to recall the points being raised by the professor.

Remember that you don't have to take down every word. You simply need enough to help you recall the point being discussed in class. Good professors often will bring information to class that supplements the information covered by the reading materials. If this is the case, make sure to take notes on these examples and supplemental materials. If you capture these examples accurately, you will have great material to study from when exam time comes.

Paraphrasing

Another good tip on note taking is to learn how to paraphrase. Paraphrasing is hearing a professor explain a point in five sentences and boiling it down to one comprehensive sentence. Paraphrasing is distilling words into your own language. Be careful. There are times when you need the very words that are being said, and paraphrasing will not suffice. You will have to decide when you should paraphrase and when you should not paraphrase.

"Taking good notes requires your effort and discipline."

To try your hand at paraphrasing, try this exercise. Read the following three paragraphs and distill them into one or two sentences.

There are many required classes. These will cover basic educational requirements that I will refer to as one hundred level classes. You will also likely encounter basic educational requirements for your major. I will begin with the one hundred level classes.

The one hundred level classes may be taken at any time during your educational career. These classes are often thought of by new students as classes that must be gotten out of the way before taking "real" classes. You should not schedule these classes together, all in one or two semesters. Save some of them for later in your academic career. For example, if you need a one hundred level health class and two one hundred level physical education classes, there is a temptation to schedule one health class and one physical education class your first semester and your second physical education class your second semester to have these classes out of the way. I would not schedule them this way.

My recommendation is to save several of these classes for later in your third and fourth year when you need an easier class to relieve the pressure. These one hundred level classes are generally easier and require less time and effort than the more advanced classes. In the example above, I might schedule one of the three classes the first year, one the second year, and save one for either my third or fourth year. Later in your college career, you will be taking more demanding classes and will appreciate an easier, one hundred level class. Also, once you have two or three years of study under your belt, these classes will prove to be even easier for you. You will be able to get a good grade with less effort than if you had scheduled it your first semester.

Your paraphrase might read: "Required classes should not all be scheduled together. Spread them out, if possible, to use later in your third or fourth year."

For more practice with this technique, try using a newspaper story again.This time, read the first three paragraphs of a front-page story. Then write in one or two sentences, if possible, what the first three paragraphs are about.

This exercise is well worth the time that it takes. It will train you to put three loaves of bread into one bag. You will also learn to recognize the important information and discard what is less important very quickly.

The point of taking notes is to get down the information that will be useful to you later. Whether you are listing information below a main point or heading, paraphrasing longer passages, or taking down theorems verbatim, your notes must be readable, in a logical outline form, and contain the information you need.

The Blank Left Page

One more note taking tip: write on the right-hand page of the notebook. There is an advantage to using only one side at this point. When you use a three-ring binder and use only the front of the page,

> "*Paraphrasing is hearing a professor explain a particular point in five sentences and boiling it down to one comprehensive sentence.*"

when you flip the page you will have a blank page on the left and your new page of notes on the right. If you continue this regimen, you will end up with blank pages facing your class notes. This gives you space to add additional information to your notes while you are studying.

Several times I have mentioned interlineating new or additional information into your notes. The blank left page will give you a place to interlineate items that will make your notes more complete. The blank left page also gives you a place to put a mark in your notes—without having to otherwise interrupt your note taking—when you want to remind yourself to ask the professor about a confusing point during his or her office hours.

Self Assessment

This chapter has been filled with chances for you to practice note-taking techniques. You have already had the chance to 1) practice taking notes in outline form; 2) practice taking down a long passage (writing down the first two or three words and the first letter of the remaining words); and 3) paraphrasing three paragraphs of material into a few sentences.

Now, I know that each of you has diligently worked through these examples as you were reading, so what follows should be considered 'extra credit' in the art of studying.

I. Practice taking notes in outline form

Read the following two paragraphs from the next chapter and create an outline from what you read.

Reviewing Notes

"Quick, recite the Pledge of Allegiance. Now sing (at least to yourself) the Star-Spangled Banner. How difficult was it to remember the words? Did you struggle? Perhaps, if you were not raised in the United States you did, but if you were raised in the U.S., you began each school day with the Pledge

Self Assessment

of Allegiance and you heard the Star-Spangled Banner at the beginning of every baseball game you ever attended. The sheer number of repetitions burned those words into your brain. Most of us could not forget them if we tried.

These two examples show us the power of repetition. If you hear something enough times, you remember it. Some of us are better auditory learners—hearing our subject matter repeated over and over again helps us retain what we hear. Others are better visual learners, while others learn best by handling or repeating the new information in some manner. Whichever you are, you will retain the new information by its repeated application in the manner that works best for you."

Self Assessment

II. Practice taking down a long passage

Have someone read the following passage and take it down, word-for-word, using the technique of writing down the first few words and then taking down the first letter of the remaining words.

Before we tackle what you should study and how you choose what is important to study and what is not, I want to address what is, in my opinion, one of the biggest mistakes young students make when it comes to studying."

III. Practice paraphrasing

Here, again, are the first three paragraphs that you read earlier in this chapter. Read these three paragraphs and distill them into one or two sentences for your notes.

Self Assessment

There are many required classes. These will cover basic educational requirements that I will refer to as one hundred level classes. You will also likely encounter basic educational requirements for your major. I will begin with the one hundred level classes.

The one hundred level classes may be taken at any time during your educational career. These classes are often thought of by new students as classes that must be gotten out of the way before taking "real" classes. You should not schedule these classes together, all in one or two semesters. Save some of them for later in your academic career. For example, if you need a one hundred level health class and two one hundred level physical education classes, there is a temptation to schedule one health class and one physical education class your first semester and your second physical education class your second semester to have these classes out of the way. I would not schedule them this way.

My recommendation is to save several of these classes for later in your third and fourth year when you need an easier class to relieve the pressure. These one hundred level classes are generally easier and require less time and effort than the more

Self Assessment

advanced classes. In the example above, I might schedule one of the three classes the first year, one the second year, and save one for either my third or fourth year. Later in your college career, you will be taking more demanding classes and will appreciate an easier, one hundred level class. Also, once you have two or three years of study under your belt, these classes will prove to be even easier for you. You will be able to get a good grade with less effort than if you had scheduled it your first semester.

CHAPTER 5

Reviewing Your Notes and Study Skills

Reviewing Notes
Study Skills
Studying vs Reading
Learning Demands Repetition
Your Daily Review
Class Preparation
Readings
Class Assignments
Where and When to Study
Time Allotted to Studying
Time Management
Avoid Time Wasters
Highlighting Notes
Study Aids
Study Groups

"To wind the mighty secrets of the past, And turn the key of time."
Henry Kirke White

This chapter covers the organization of your study materials, reviewing your notes, study habits, and everything right up to test preparation. These areas are all inextricably linked. You need to learn to manage your assignments and responsibilities for each class in a structured manner and to be able to review that information in an efficient way.

Overview of the Entire Semester
Your Study Calendar

Creating an overview of your entire semester during the first week of classes is essential. This keeps you from being surprised later in the semester when you discover that you have three mid-term exams in two days, or some similar crisis. I suggest either making your own calendar or purchasing one that has ample space for you to write in your assignments, your tests, and any other relevant information. I found that creating my own monthly calendar for the entire semester using a ruler, pen, and a blank piece of paper had a **cathartic** effect on me, giving me the sense of truly shaping the future of each semester myself.

Your calendar must include these essentials for the entire semester:

a) Your reading assignments for every day (or as much of the semester as each professor's syllabus covers)

b) Any tests, including regularly scheduled quizzes or chapter tests

c) Any papers or projects that are due, including dates that rough drafts or proposals are due

d) Breaks, such as spring break, holidays, and days you know you will not be attending classes, such as religious holidays

e) Days when certain resources or professors are not available,and

f) Finals

There is a basic example of a calendar for one month's worth of studies on page 75.

It is important that your calendar be filled out for the entire semester as soon as reasonably possible. You will receive ONE grade at the end of the semester for each class and that grade will reflect the work you did for the entire semester. You need to think globally about each of your decisions in each class. Everything you do or fail to do affects your entire semester and your final grade.

Obviously, you will not know all the information mentioned

above on the first day. Some of the information will have to be added as your semester progresses. The point is to have one place to gather ALL the pertinent information from all your classes. There are several benefits to having one academic calendar.

First, by being able to view all your class assignments on one calendar, you will be able to anticipate when you will be very busy. If, for example, you notice that you have both a Shakespeare paper and a Biology project due on the 14th and you have a test in World Religions on the 15th, you may want to try to finish either your Biology or Shakespeare project a day early to give you a little more time to study for your World Religions test. By putting everything on one calendar you spot the logjams before they occur and have the chance to act accordingly.

Second, you can put in your own deadlines to further assist you. Using the earlier example, you may want to put on your calendar "ROUGH DRAFT OF SHAKESPEARE PAPER" on the 7th and have the paper ready to hand in on the 14th. In this way, you are managing your time effectively.

Finally, you are taking control of your single most precious commodity—your time. You can purchase more study aids and buy better notebooks, but you cannot purchase more time. We all have the same amount of time. The question is, how do we spend it? Putting everything on one calendar will help you decide where you can best invest your time.

By committing everything to one study calendar, you also make a conscious decision to be **cognizant** of your academic responsibilities. You are sending a signal to yourself that studying is important and deserves the proper amount of attention. You are molding your own character with your choices. Choosing to be more responsible for your studies is a mature way of addressing your academic career.

Your calendar will also be your ally when you need to decide if you can afford the time for that two-day holiday with your friends. You can check your calendar and see what your educational workload is and decide accordingly. You can also use your calendar to plan ahead and make changes in the three days preceding your two-day holiday to facilitate taking time off.

This brings up another very useful point. If you need to take time away from your study routine, whether it is two hours or two days, plan accordingly. If you know that you will be missing an entire evening's study time, don't look at your schedule and say, "Yes, I have time to make this up afterwards. I can double-up my reviewing time the next night and make up for it." Instead, do your doubling-up BEFORE the missed time. In this way you will not fall behind, and you will give yourself a real break.

> *"By committing everything to one study calendar, you also make a conscious decision to be cognizant of your academic responsibilities."*

Keeping to your routine is essential! Falling behind in high school is one thing. Falling behind in college is something else altogether. There comes a point beyond which no amount of studying will help you catch up. By studying before you take your hiatus you assure that you will not fall behind. And, you give yourself a real break from your routine.

When you spend your time doing anything other than what you should be doing (in your case studying), you feel guilty. Ask students who have stolen time away from their study routine without first making adequate reparations to their schedule. They will tell you that they did not enjoy the time away nearly as much as they had hoped because of the guilt they felt. This guilt is your conscience telling you "You should be studying." Why take this extra guest named Guilt with you? Do the extra studying beforehand and you will have an answer, should Guilt tap you on the shoulder.

Reviewing Notes

Quick, recite the Pledge of Allegiance. Now sing (at least to yourself) the Star-Spangled Banner. How difficult was it to remember the words? Did you struggle? Perhaps, if you were not raised in the United States you did, but if you were raised in the U.S., you began each school day with the Pledge of Allegiance and you heard the Star-Spangled Banner at the beginning of every baseball game you ever attended. The sheer number of repetitions burned those words into your brain. Most of us could not forget them if we tried.

These two examples show us the power of repetition. If you hear something enough times, you remember it. Some of us are better auditory learners—hearing our subject matter repeated over and over again helps us retain what we hear. Others are better visual learners, while others learn best by handling or repeating the new information in some manner. Whichever you are, you will retain the new information by its repeated application in the manner that works best for you.

Study Skills

The next time someone tries to give you advice about studying, be sure to ask how well their "system" worked for them. There are as many systems and tricks out there as there are universities and colleges in America. My experience is that many students claim to look for a system that helps them learn when what they are really trying to find is a way to get a good grade on a test without doing the work. Becoming a good student takes work and dedication. The topics covered in this chapter will point out pitfalls that hurt many students and will point you in the right direction to get the most out of your study time. Your success is still up to you.

Studying vs. Reading

Before we tackle what you should study and how you choose what is important to study and what is not, I want to address what is, in my opinion, one of the biggest mistakes young students make when it comes to studying. Students often mistake simple reading for studying. Let me explain. Students often do not comprehend that simply reading a section of text or simply doing the one or two assigned problems from a section in a math book is insufficient for them to truly master the material. Too often, students are more concerned with getting finished so they can get on to other things than they are with mastering the material.

Any time you begin studying a subject, your goal should be that you will "own" the material when you are done. By owning the material, I mean that you must know it and understand it as well as your own address or telephone number. To say you want to learn material "well enough to pass the test," especially early in the semester, is a huge mistake, and is setting your goals far too low. Set your goals high. No one will do this for you. You can achieve so much more in life if you set your sights high and refuse to settle for second-best.

If you do not own the material and know it inside-out and upside-down, you will not have a good foundation from which to move forward. You can read through your assignment to meet your minimum responsibility, but if you have not understood it or taken the time to thoroughly grasp each of the concepts, you will fall short when it comes time to apply the information you have read.

If you were learning to play baseball for the first time and you never really learned how to throw the ball with accuracy, it would be a waste of time to work with you on "hitting the cut-off man" from the outfield on an extra-base hit. You can't hit the side of a barn, let alone a more intricate play like hitting the cut-off man. Your lack of "owning" the basics would stop you from learning more about baseball.

Studying academic material is very similar. You must own the basics before you can go on and master the more difficult material. Merely reading the assignment may not be enough.

You need to view each class as part of a progressive journey, with the first step being the requirement for the second step, and the second step being the requirement for the third step, and so on. Look at each section of your textbook and each week of your class as another step. Tell yourself, "I cannot advance to the next step until I have mastered this one."

Learning Demands Repetition

You may have heard the old **axiom** that "Teaching demands repetition." The only reason that teaching demands repetition is that learning demands repetition. If we could all hear or read something once and then know it and own it as our own, teaching would not demand repetition. But most of us are not built that way. We need to hear things over and over, sometimes in more than one way, to fully grasp a new idea, concept, or skill.

Those persons who are blessed with photographic memories will tell you that simply being able to recall material photographically does not in itself end their task of learning. I attended law school with a very bright student who had a photographic memory. This student had to study to understand and synthesize the material just like the rest of us. A photographic memory can make a difference, but learning is more than simple recall.

The real question in learning is what information should you repeat; on what should you spend your time?

Whatever subject you are studying, the notes you have taken in class—along with any materials your professor has handed out to you—are the foundation from which you should study. See chapter three on Note Taking for a more thorough discussion of this subject. You need to use your notes as your map to success for each class.

I suggest a multi-level approach to studying and reviewing. This approach includes both repetition and synthesis.

Your Daily Review
First Level

Your class notes are likely chronological, following your daily class calendar. I suggest that each day you go over that day's notes, one class at a time, line by line, until you can recite them in either word-for-word form if the material requires it (as in knowing the chemical compounds) or in paraphrased or synopsis form. You should continue to go over the first page of each day's notes until you are able to recall the material accurately without peeking. I always used a piece of paper to slide down the page as I went. I would cover the page and recite what each topic was and what the professor had said about it. Once you have mastered the first page of your notes, move on to the second page, and so on, until you have thoroughly reviewed that day's notes.

"The only reason that teaching demands repetition is that learning demands repetition."

If you happen to be in a class that does not require you to take notes, you can use the same approach using your textbook as review material.

Second Level

Review the main concepts or topics that were covered. This step should follow your daily review and only takes a fraction of the time of your daily review. You should try to think of the big picture of what you are studying and try to see how the pieces you are reviewing fit into the subject as a whole.

For this level of review, you may want to write out the concepts or topics. You may be able to fit them into the outline, or you may simply want to list them, as you are able to recall them. Don't get bogged down in the details of how you put this information together at this point. The very act of recalling the information will form an internal organization in your mind. You should be able to do this without looking at your notes, though that may not always be the case.

At this level you are beginning to synthesize the material from class. You are no longer simply spitting out what you have memorized but are beginning to put it together in some cohesive way. Writing it down will force you to work with the material in a way that just thinking about it does not accomplish. This step will only take a few moments but will pay huge dividends if done regularly. Remember that you will recall more of what you write down than what you only hear or say.

Third Level

Now that you have mastered the material from your class notes to a fairly high level, add in any additional materials that your professor has given you. This could be a handout or a reading assignment from an outside source. Add this material using the methods outlined in the First and Second Levels, giving it as much attention as the professor suggested you give it. These materials are usually the "gravy" that makes the material more interesting. I once had a professor suggest that after our class read Shakespeare's Taming of the Shrew, we should view a particular version of it. The version he suggested to us (which happened to feature John Cleese of Monty Python fame) has become one of my favorites and presented a wonderfully entertaining evening for my whole family. I gained a great deal from watching it. Don't ignore your professor's "suggested" materials. My experience has been that these are often the most enlightening materials of all.

Fourth Level

Once you have reviewed today's materials, take a few moments to review the prior day's notes in abbreviated fashion. Go over each page of each previous day's notes, this time spending less time on the small details than on the material as a whole. If you have spent sufficient time memorizing and synthesizing in the preceding days, this exercise will not take long and will serve to reinforce what you have already learned.

You may be thinking that this multi-level method of reviewing takes too much time. You're wrong. It takes discipline and a desire to succeed. The fact is that disorganized reviewing and studying takes a great deal more effort and time and yields fewer results. If you only study "when the spirit moves you" and without a plan, you tend to study frantically, trying to cover too much at once and with worry and fear as your chief motivators. Disciplined reviewing, as set out above, gives you a framework for studying and has personal excellence as its motivation.

By now you may be saying, "That's all well and good for reviewing yesterday's classes, but what about tomorrow's classes?" Studying your notes from yesterday's and last week's classes are the backbone of your daily routine. But that is not all there is to being a good student. You must also be looking forward. We will next look at the work and time you need to put into preparing for tomorrow's classes.

Class Preperation

Class preparation will likely take up a significant percentage of your study time each evening. I shared the section on reviewing class notes first for several reasons.

First, daily reviewing of notes is the single most overlooked study habit I know. EVERYONE knows that you should do tomorrow's homework, whether it's reading or writing or preparing a speech or a presentation. The consequences of NOT completing homework for tomorrow's class are felt immediately. If you do not hand in an assignment, you get a zero or some reduction on the assignment.

Also, coming to class without being minimally prepared carries a certain negative stigma, though not nearly what it was years ago. For these two reasons, most students will make some effort at class preparation. Few, however, take any time to review class notes from classes gone by. There are no immediate consequences for skipping a daily review. In fact, the consequences do not show up until testing time. It is easy to brush aside a daily review, as it does not fit neatly into society's instant gratification model. To tackle the daily review takes foresight and planning, something too few students possess.

Finally, there is no negative stigma attached to failing to do a daily review. On the contrary, a student who disciplines himself to a study routine is often in the minority. Don't let the negative impressions of others stop you from making the most of your education. The daily review is the backbone of your knowledge in each class. Stay focused on the goal of achieving your best!

So, what about class preparation? There are a few things you should know.

Readings

Read your assignments. Don't ever let yourself get caught behind in your reading assignments. Make a plan and stick to it.

If you will turn to the sample calendar on page 75, you will notice that I have included the chapters or sections that are due for each day. Use your calendar as your daily guide for how much you need to read. In my own case, I am a very slow reader. My own study calendar was always marked up with even more detailed notes about what to read

> *"Disciplined reviewing . . . has personal excellence as its motivation."*

and when to have it read. For example, I would break down items like "Midsummer Night's Dream" by page numbers and note on my calendar which pages I had to have read for each day of the week. This was the only way I could keep up with the assigned readings.

Also, if there are supplemental readings that are suggested but not required, don't take the time to read the supplemental materials until you have read the required materials. These materials are called "required" for a reason.

Use a Dictionary

Expanding your vocabulary is one of the best things you can do for yourself, whether or not you are a student. Communication skills are of vital importance to everyone. By expanding your vocabulary, you are expanding your ability to communicate with the world.

When you come to a word with which you are unfamiliar, stop and look it up. I know it takes time and I understand that it is sometimes a pain, but you must get used to learning as a way of life while you are in college. If you are reading a required text, then assume that this is a "required word" for you to understand. There is no better way to expand your vocabulary than to learn unfamiliar words in context. You have already seen this exercise in action. If you don't know what I'm talking about, go back and read the introduction of this book.

Class Assignments

Hand in all your assignments on time. If you use your study calendar to record when your assignments are due, you will never be caught short, unable to hand in an assignment on time (unless something unforeseen or drastic occurs that is outside of your control). By class assignments, I mean anything your professor expects you to hand in. If your professor assigns it, then have it ready to hand in on time. Don't allow yourself any other choice!

Extra Credit

Consider every extra credit opportunity you have as if it is a regular class assignment that must be handed in to your professor. By considering the extra credit as part of your regular assignments, you create an expectation of completing and earning this credit. What harm can it do for you to attempt to earn all the extra credit available? Don't make the "I don't have the time" excuse just yet— you are presently reading a book that is not on any professor's required reading list (as far as I know). You had time for this, didn't you? You deemed reading this book important enough to invest the time. Think the same way about extra credit.

Where and When to Study

This is another good point that, though intuitive, is still worth discussing for a moment. Choose your study location carefully. I don't recommend studying in any room that has easy access to a television or a computer. Turn off your cell phone when you are studying. (That's the little button that keeps it silent—on purpose! Ha ha)

Also, don't try to study in any environment where you know you have a good chance of being interrupted. Seek out a quiet location that is well suited for studying. This is usually a library, though some college campus libraries are more like sushi bars without the raw fish.

I liked studying in the library at my college, particularly on the top floor, as it was often a little warmer than the other floors and not many people wanted to study there. I would simply dress comfortably and have the place to myself.

Use your common sense. Choose a study location that will enhance your studying and will allow you to focus on your materials, not your surroundings.

As for what time of day is best to study, again, this is fairly intuitive. Do not study when you are likely to have trouble staying awake (like too early in the morning if you are not a morning person or too late at night if you are not a night person). Look at your schedule and balance your class schedule, study time, and work schedule so that you have ample time to study.

This raises the question, how much time is ample time?

Time Allotted to Studying

One of the smartest things you can do is allot yourself ample time to go over your notes from class, as discussed in the previous section. But how much time is enough? The answer depends upon many variables, such as how fast you read, how much you retain from one reading to the next, how long your attention span is, and how tired you are. The amount of time you need is also partly a function of the subject you are studying. Complex materials are generally absorbed better in large, mass studying times. More mundane materials, even substantial amounts, are generally learned and retained better in multiple, shorter study sessions.

There is no set answer to the question how much time is enough. I suggest that you begin with a simple ratio of time spent in the classroom versus time spent outside of the classroom studying the material. In law school, the rule of thumb is that three hours of study are required for every hour spent in class. If you have a one-hour class in Contracts, it will likely take you three hours or more to prepare for that class. Most secondary education generally requires less time, usually closer to a two-to-one ratio. If you are in high school preparing for college, I suggest you use a one-to-one ratio during your remaining time in high school. If you have a forty-five-minute class in French, spend at least forty-five minutes in preparation for your next French class.

The controlling factor of time spent studying is mastery of the material. Spend as much time as it takes for you to master the material. I mentioned that I was a slow reader. In the English department of my university, the expectation of the faculty was that students should be able to read one page per minute with good comprehension. I could not read nearly that quickly and still cannot do so. At that time, I read a little less than half that speed. That meant it took me longer to read and longer to study; therefore, I required longer study periods. I could have justified shortening my studying time by saying, "I'm spending way too long on this, twice as long as my classmates . . . better knock off for now," but I didn't. And you shouldn't either! Make excelling at your school work your measuring rod. Spend as long as you need to in order to master the material.

Time Management

There are entire volumes devoted to time management. I am not trying to supplant that wisdom in these few pages. I simply want to give you a few hints that, taken with the other materials from this chapter, will assist you in making the most of your study time.

There are a few simple steps that you must know to become an effective academic time manager. I call them the "Three A P's" of time management: Assess, Assess, Assume, and Prioritize.

Assess

First: Assess. You must accurately <u>assess how much time</u> you need to devote to studying. Be cognizant of what is truly important and what items in your schedule can wait. I remember how amazed I was to discover that many students could find time to watch their favorite TV show and do a little bar-hopping but could never seem to find the time to thoroughly study before class. Assess your schedule before you make the decision about how much time you need to study. Make a quality decision as to how much time you will devote to studying and how much free time you will allot yourself.

By deciding ahead of time that you will spend a set amount of time studying each evening, you will be "pre-deciding" time management questions before they arise. This is precisely what you MUST do. You must decide that your studying time is an appointment that you cannot break. Once you do so, you will have fewer time conflicts. Here's an example:

At the beginning of the semester you decide that you will need to spend three hours studying each weekday evening, and that you can routinely spend from seven pm to ten pm studying. If someone invites you to see a movie on a weekday evening, and the movie begins at eight-thirty pm, you already know that you are unavailable because you already have something important to do. Does this mean you can't see any movies until the end of the semester? Of course not. It does mean, however, that you may need to wait until the weekend, or that you may need to do extra studying the day before to keep from falling behind.

> "There is no set answer to the question how much time is enough."

The point of this example is clear—you must assess how much time you need to study and make the quality decision that you are going to spend that time studying. It takes a decision, your commitment, and discipline. You can do it.

Assess

Second: <u>Assess what you need to study</u>. You will find that most of your study time will be routine if you implement a daily review of your notes. There will be times, however, when you need to spend extra time on one subject because of a test or large project. The point is that you need to assess each day's reviewing in light of your upcoming assignments and tests. You will occasionally need to adjust your routine, and at other times you will simply need to expand the amount of time allotted for studying.

One additional word of advice here: Once you have decided on a routine of study, stick to it. It is easy to set aside the daily review in order to take care of class assignments or other class projects. Don't allow this to happen to you. I have read that it takes twenty-one consecutive days to create a habit. Your daily review is the backbone or your academic success. Invest the time and make studying a habit. If you find that you must consistently set aside your daily review in favor of class assignments, then you need to adjust your schedule accordingly. You need more time for your daily review.

Assume

Third: Assume. <u>Assume that some of the review will take you longer than you would like</u>. Assume that you will be interrupted and that you will have to extend your review and study sessions to make up for lost time. Assume that a friend will ask you to spend your regular studying time doing something that you would love to do. If you don't assume these things, then it means that you areassuming that your study time will work out exactly as you planned it. That is unlikely to happen, so you are better off preparing for other contingencies by assuming they will happen.

Prioritize

<u>Finally: Prioritize. This is simple, I know, but one Tuesday night when you are faced</u> with a French test Wednesday that is thirty-three percent of your grade and a paper in English due Thursday and another test in another subject on the same Thursday, you will be glad you spent some time prioritizing.

When prioritizing your study time, look at your tests first, your assignments second, any large projects that are out of the ordinary third, and your daily reviewing fourth. This does not mean your reviewing is least important. In my opinion, your daily reviewing is the most important overall study strategy you will take from this chapter. If you have an upcoming test, however, you need to spend an ample amount of time preparing for that test.

Look at all you have to do one day at a time, and make a conscious decision as to what is most important, then what is secondarily important, and so on. Allot your time accordingly.

Academic time management is much the same as other time management.

- You need to assess how much time you need, assess what needs to be done,
- assume that everything will not always go as you plan it, and
- properly prioritize your studies.

You will be able to complete your tasks to the highest degree of excellence you can muster. These are the Three A P's in action!

Avoid Time Wasters

There are a **plethora** of time wasters that would like to steal your time. The internet and television are two obvious time wasters that have been responsible for lowering more than their share of grades among today's students. But these are the obvious ones. What about the more subtle time wasters?

Reading as opposed to studying, as discussed earlier, can be a time waster. Instead of digging into your notes and your text to try and truly understand a subject, you mindlessly read the text or outline and call it studying. The **recalcitrant** student says, "But I studied," after doing poorly on a test. The truth is that little if any effort was put into studying for that test. The student simply made sure that his or her eyes did indeed scan the black ink on the white paper. There was no learning going on. Learning takes a decision and commitment. Mindless reading can be a huge time waster.

> "Make a quality decision as to how much time you will devote to studying and how much free time you will allot yourself."

Another time waster is what I like to call the "I'm getting organized" procrastinator. I know all about this one because this is a time waster that I must guard against all the time. This student justifies spending half her time in organizing notes, putting together another new schedule, recovering a book for class, and writing out all the assignments again, in both her notebooks, just to be organized. The truth is, the student does not want to knuckle down to do the demanding work of studying, and make no mistake about it, studying is demanding work. He or she spends time doing what looks like good academic work that is preparatory in nature in place of studying. These students will often complain that they would have done better on the test or assignment if they'd only had "more time." There is a need for organizing learning and studying materials, but it is minimal in comparison to the time necessary for effective studying.

Another matter that can cause your study time to be less effective is what I call "picking at nits." I grew up in an area where a "nitpicker" was a person who would strain to understand a small bit of information, usually something insignificant, while missing the larger point altogether. For example, the person who is obsessed by rearranging pictures so that they are perfectly straight on a sinking ship is a "nitpicker."

In studying, you need to be able to know when a point is important and when it is a "nit" of information that is inconsequential. I once tried to study with a group of friends in law school who had elevated nit-picking to a new level. After one or two study sessions, we came to a mutual understanding that we should not study together. They wanted to pull apart every jot and title in the name of thoroughness, and I wanted to get the main points during our joint study time and leave the smaller, more detailed learning to private sessions. Nit-picking every minor point will slow you down and will not, in the end, add much to your learning or to your final grades. The word of caution here is not to use "I don't want to be a nitpicker" as an excuse to not study or memorize critical information. Sometimes such information is tedious and there is no other way to learn it than by rote memorization. Just don't nit-pick details that are of little or no value to your overall learning. It will only slow you down.

Highlighting Notes

There is a long-held belief that marking notes with a highlighter assists in learning new material. While I believe this to be dubious, I will acknowledge that it may help to call your attention to the highlighted item later. The question is when to highlight and what to highlight.

Occasionally your teacher or professor will say something like, "Now pay attention because this is likely to show up on your test." When you are doing your daily review, you may want to highlight or underline those items that you have reason to believe will be on your test. This way, when you begin to use those same notes to review for your test, you will not have to try to remember what the teacher said would likely be on the test. It will be highlighted in your notes.

One cautionary word on highlighting and underlining. Some students mistake highlighting for learning, thinking that the very act of highlighting somehow magically makes that passage or phrase more important for them. This is false. All highlighting does is call your attention to the passage at some later time. You still need to go back and spend the appropriate amount of time with the material so that you can master it. I had one friend who had five or six different colors that she used to highlight her textbooks. There was a veritable rainbow in each of her books. I don't believe that it ever assisted her in any tangible way. It simply made her feel better.

Study Aids

Study aids such as **mnemonics** are wonderful and should be used as necessary. But be careful—mnemonics are ways to help you study, not substitutes for true learning. If you find a book that is titled "How to get straight A's using these three simple tricks," I would recommend you not read it! The rightful place of technology as study aids is also addressed in the final chapter of this book. I otherwise relegate study aids such as mnemonics to test and final preparations, as I believe that is where they are best utilized.

> *"Nit-picking every minor point will slow you down and will not, in the end, add much to your learning or to your final grades."*

Study Groups

Students attending a common class will sometimes decide to study together. An innate feeling of safety in numbers, as well as the camaraderie of facing the unknown together, make study groups inviting, especially since most students in college are away from home for the first time. This smaller group promises students another safe place to gather.

Ideally, a study group is made up of students who pull their own weight and contribute equally to the dynamics of the group. If you ever find a study group like this, please contact me immediately. A woolly mammoth sighting is more likely! Perhaps I overstate the problem, but I have been a student for years and I have rarely found a study group that lives up to the ideal.

If you decide to study for a class with other students, I suggest that you lay out the ground rules at the outset. This limits the confusion and hurt feelings that can crop up at the end of a semester.

You might decide that you are only going to review daily notes together. The purpose of this type of group would be to help ensure that you did not miss or misunderstand any of the information from that day. Each study session with the group might last only fifteen or twenty minutes,

> *"Learning takes a decision and commitment. Mindless reading can be a huge time waster."*

but you may find that the little insights that each person brings to the group will add to your overall understanding of the material.

Conversely, you might decide that your study group is going to meet weekly to review the notes from the week. Fine, as long as everyone is attending and participating. If you have members who consistently cannot make the study sessions, but who would like a copy of your notes or your group outline near the end of the semester, you have a dilemma. These are the types of problems that are, unfortunately, typical of study groups.

Choosing your study group partners is a difficult task. On the one hand, you want to get your group started as early in the semester as possible to get the most out of the experience. On the other hand, at the beginning of the semester you do not know the students in class well enough to be able to tell the rocket scientists from the space cadets! I suggest you wait a few weeks so that you can make a more informed choice.

So, what if you get into a study group and you find that it is not helping you? When do you cut and run? There is no easy answer here. You must decide how to best use your time. Don't allow a group that wastes your time to drag you down.

Sun.	Monday	Tuesday	Wed.	Thursday	Friday	Sat.
29	30	1	2	3	4	5
	Shakespeare Finish Macbeth Micro Biology txt: pgs 30-44	World Rel. read C5-pg.70 Symbolic Logic chapter review with problems	Shakespeare Macbeth review: Begin king lear Micro Biology meet in lab Phys Ed. @ gym	Shakespeare king Lear finish Symbolic Logic chapter review problem	Micro Biology lecture Phys. Ed @ gym	
6	7	8	9	10	11	12
	Shakespeare DRAFT of PAPER Finish king lear Micro Biology text 45-62 Pt B: C 1-5	World Rel. read C6-pg.98 Symbolic Logic chapter four with problems	Shakespeare K Lear discussion Micro Biology meet in lab Phys Ed. @ gym	Shakespeare Begins Mid S.N. World Religions read to end of ch. 6 prepare for test! Symbolic Logic begin ch. 5 QUIZ TODAY	Micro Biology lecture Phys. Ed @ field house FINAL DRAFT of Macbeth paper Due Monday!	
13	14	15	16	17	18	19
	Shakespeare Paper DUE read first 2 acts Micro Biology project due meet in lab today	World Rel. TEST Ch 4-6 Symbolic Logic chapter five with problems	Shakespeare Finish Mid S.N. Micro Biology meet in lab Phys Ed. @ field house	Shakespeare Mid S.N. World Religions read Ch 7 to 133 Symbolic Logic begin ch. 7 QUIZ TODAY	Micro Biology CANCELED Phys. Ed @ CANCELED begin Much Ado	
20	21	22	23	24	25	26
	Shakespeare Much Ado first 3 acts Micro Biology text 80-94 Pt B: E1-4	World Rel. read to end of ch 7 Symbolic Logic chapter six with problems	Shakespeare Finish Much Ado Micro Biology meet in lab Phys Ed. @ gym	Shakespeare Comedies World Religions read Ch 8 to 130 Symbolic Logic begin ch. 7 QUIZ TODAY	Micro Biology lecture Phys. Ed @ gym	
27	28	29	30	31	1	2
	Shakespeare Venus & Adonis Micro Biology text 63-80 Pt B: D - all problems	World Rel. finish Ch 8 review for test Symbolic Logic chapter seven with problems Midterm next week!	Shakespeare Venus Micro Biology meet in lab Phys Ed. @ gym	Shakespeare Sonnets: 7,9-60 World Religions read entire Ch 9 Symbolic Logic begin ch. 7 QUIZ TODAY	Micro Bio lecture Phys. Ed @ gym	

Self Assessment

Chapter Five covered a lot of ground. For this chapter's self assessment, I'm going to give you a little pop quiz to see if you were paying attention to what you were reading.

1. I should plan for my upcoming semester

   a) by hoping that I don't have two tests on the same day at any time during the semester.

   b) around the concert tickets I can get my hands on.

   c) by creating a study schedule that includes my entire semester.

   d) by sleeping in as much as possible.

2. The biggest difference between quality studying and simply reading is that

   a) my eyes get more bloodshot when I study.

   b) studying requires that I actually think while I read.

   c) reading can be done while both slightly and thoroughly inebriated.

   d) studying requires dedication to academic excellence while simple reading does not.

3. The reason that teaching demands repetition is that

   a) most students don't listen the first time through.

   b) learning demands repetition.

   c) most teachers don't get it the first time through, either.

   d) most teachers are paid by the word, not the hour.

Self Assessment

4. You should review your class notes

   a) when the spirit moves you.

   b) at least 36 hours before your finals.

   c) daily.

   d) more often than you watch Saturday Night Live.

5. Class preparation includes all the following except

   a) arriving on time.

   b) reading the assignments.

   c) bringing the teacher a nice, shiny apple.

   d) completing your homework on time.

6. In order to expand your ability to communicate with the world effectively, you should

   a) increase your Facebook presence.

   b) Snapchat without ceasing.

   c) use a dictionary, especially when you come upon a word you do not know.

   d) just pretend you understand the really big words.

7. Studying is best done

   a) at your favorite watering hole.

   b) while simultaneously watching TV and talking on the phone.

   c) in a quiet place where you will be undisturbed.

   d) while holding your breath.

Self Assessment

8. The "three A P's" of studying stand for

a) Always Assume a Passing grade.

b) Away, Away, Away old Pauli girl.

c) Assess, Assess, Assume and Prioritize.

d) After an Avalanche an Aardvark Prances.

9. Studying in the keg room at a fraternity party could be considered

a) bad time management.

b) bad beer management.

c) a major time waster when it comes to studying.

d) all of the above.

10. The best way to ensure that you do the best you can in each of your classes is to

a) learn to write small so that you can inscribe notes on the inside of your eyelids at test time.

b) offer to paint your professor's house, for FREE!

c) get friendly with the smartest kid in the class and then steal her notes.

d) review your class notes daily.

CHAPTER 6

Tests

Tests should be fun!
When Should I Begin Studying?
Steps to Preparing for a Test
Don't Leave Anything to Chance
Nothing Beats Repetition
Don't Try to Outguess the Professor
Mnemonics, Associations, and Anagrams
Stay Focused
Don't Reinvent the Wheel
Timing Isn't Everything, but It's Important
Post-mortem

"Measure not the work until the day's out and the labor done."
Elizabeth Barrett Browning

L ike it or not, most of us have our academic acumen measured by test grades. Some of us are good test takers while others are not. Certain students do very well on standardized tests but fare poorly when it comes to essays. Others are just the opposite. Whether you are a good test taker or a bad test taker, you can improve and get better grades on your tests.

As a slight aside, if you require assistance with answering essay questions, I recommend the book *College Writing with Readings* by Jonathan Langon. I have seen no better text to assist the high school or college student in mastering the skill of paragraph and essay writing. If you can write a good essay, you will do well on written exams that require essay answers.

Tests Should Be Fun

There are several things you need to consider about tests. First, you should look at tests as the fun part of your education. That's right, the fun part. Throughout the entire semester you have to sit and listen to what somebody else says about a subject. Now it's your turn to say what you think and show how much you know about that subject.

You are likely asking by now, "But what about the stress, the tension of having to do well on the test, or not knowing what the questions will be?" I want to deal with these two issues one at a time.

First, the stress. Not all stress is bad. You need some stress to motivate you to perform. Without any stress at all, many of us would not get off the couch. Stress, in proper doses aimed in the right direction, can be a great motivator. I once had a friend in seminary who asked his professor about having butterflies in his stomach before he preached, to which the professor replied, "It's okay to have butterflies; the trick is to get them to fly in formation." Think of pre-test stress that way. Get your butterflies to fly in formation and use their energy to your benefit.

Next, let's talk about what makes tests seem so stressful—the fear of the unknown. Fear of the unknown is one of the most common fears each of us faces. A test's content can only be truly unknown to the student who does not pay attention in class or does not review his or her notes on a regular basis. If you apply yourself and routinely review and study throughout the semester, you will greatly reduce the X factor of the unknown and thereby reduce the fear of the unknown. By the time your test rolls around, your reviewing will have prepared you thoroughly for whatever the professor puts on the test. Give yourself credit. You have greatly lessened the fear of the unknown because of your diligent study habits.

Finally, let's address the importance students place on test results. Students often say things like, "I cannot afford to fail this test," or "I'm really dead if I don't get at least a high B on this test." I have had those same feelings, and I know how real they can be. Then, one day before a test, it dawned on me to compare the consequences of performing badly on a test and performing badly in the "real world."

If you perform badly on a test in college, you will get a test paper back from your professor with red marks all over it and find yourself a little further behind in that class or in that semester. That is about the extent of it. It is not a desirable place to be in, no doubt, but rarely does one bad grade so negatively impact you that you cannot recover within a reasonable amount of time.

If, however, you perform badly in life, such as by not making enough money to pay your monthly bills, you are in much bigger trouble. Yes, you still may be able to slide by, but the ramifications are much more serious. You cannot live and work comfortably carrying a load of debt. It will be a weight around your neck every time you try to make any substantial financial transaction. Neither one is desirable, but the ramifications of failing in life are greater than the ramifications of failing a test. Don't blow it out of proportion.

When Should I Begin Studying?

If you want to learn to think differently about tests, memorize this: *During my entire academic career, I only have one test—the next one.*

There is only one test within your immediate control. The NEXT ONE. As such, your upcoming test deserves most of your attention. Too simple? Not a chance. Studying academic material is challenging work and you need to simplify it every chance you get. The ideas and strategies I am sharing with you will assist you in doing your best on tests.

If you have been routinely reviewing your notes, then fully half of your work is already completed, and maybe more, depending on how seriously you have been taking your daily review time. The daily review is the basic building block of mastering any academic subject. The remainder of this chapter will look at the steps you need to take to prepare for a test in a structured way.

I am **reticent** to suggest a set schedule about how far in advance you should begin each phase of studying for a test. There are too many variables at work to give you a rigid schedule of when to begin your first overview and when you should have your final review completed. A far better way to approach timing is for you to ask yourself these questions for each test:

- How well do I know this subject?
- How much time do I have until the test?
- How much weight does this test hold?

Once you have determined the answers to these questions, you need to do your own time/benefits analysis and determine when to begin studying and when to have each component of your test preparation completed. Only you can answer these questions for each test that you face, and you will need to ask these three questions for every test you take. The answers will give you a good feel for how soon you need to begin studying.

Concerning how much weight to give a particular test or topic, I recall a test where many of the students spent a great deal of time studying something called "future interests" without really weighing how important the issue was in the overall scheme of things. Our professor had pointed out that there would be two future interest questions on the test and that, together, the two questions would be worth approximately 4 or 5 percent of the total grade. He also mentioned to us that if we put forth minimal effort, we would be given at least half-credit for each question.

I studied future interests and understood them about as well as the majority of my class. I decided not to spend any additional time trying to fine-tune my knowledge in this area, as it was not worth the extra effort. The two future interest questions on our exam were worth two and three points, respectively. I knew the answer to the two-point question and had an educated guess on the second question. I spent less than five minutes on these two questions and received four of five possible points. I am not convinced that I would have gotten all five points if I had spent an additional twenty hours studying this subject. This is a good example of knowing how much time to spend studying a topic for a test.

Once you have answered the three questions above, you are ready to begin studying for your test. Below, we will go through each of the steps to prepare you for a test.

Let me take a moment to point out that the test preparation suggestions in this chapter may seem awkward now, but once you incorporate them into your own routine of studying and adjust them to suit your own personality and way of studying, they will become second nature. I compare it to a golf swing. The first time you are taught to swing a golf club, it seems like the most awkward thing in the world. But once you have done it a few dozen times, it becomes more natural. Studying for your tests will become as natural to you as a golf swing is to a pro.

Steps to Preparing for a Test

There are several components to preparing for a test.
The components include:

1. Your daily reviews
2. First overview of the material on this test (Create a working test outline)
3. Second overview, in detail, noting your strengths and weaknesses
4. Final review
5. Brief post-mortem

Daily and Weekly Review

This topic has been covered in detail already. I cannot stress enough the importance of reviewing your class notes regularly. Without regular review, you will go from crisis to crisis, trying to cram into a few days everything that you could have been learning all semester long.

From this point on in discussing test preparation, I am going to assume that you have routinely reviewed your notes.

First Overview of the Material for this Test

You already have a good, basic understanding of the material that will be on your test from your daily reviews. You may not know the material as well as you would like, but compared to most students who don't discipline themselves to regular reviewing, you are way, way ahead of the game. The basis of knowledge that you have gained from a daily review of your notes will permit you to move forward confidently toward the test date. Remember, tests are the place to have fun by showing what you know!

Your next step is to do an overview of all the material that will be on your test.

If you have not been reviewing daily and you are reading this to prepare for an upcoming test, don't panic. You may still be able to do well on your test. You simply will not have the basis of knowledge to begin with that others have. You will have to try to study yourself into the knowledge that the daily reviewer already has. You should only take this as a warning to begin reviewing your notes daily from now on!

At this point in your test preparation, you are doing an overview, not a point-by-point rehashing of everything you know. Think of it like a physical overview of a city. If you wanted to see Pittsburgh,

Pennsylvania, you could fly over it and have an overview of the city. You might come away saying, "I want to see what that big tower over there is, and I would like to see the place where the rivers come together." The overview gives you a general lay of the land. Only a closer inspection would reveal that the big tower was the University of Pittsburgh's "Cathedral of Learning" and that the spot where the three rivers come together is called "The Point."

Your first overview must include more than just your daily class notes. Look over your textbook, any handouts that you have received, your homework assignments and quizzes, whether or not they were graded, and any other pertinent information that relates to your class.

I recommend that, at this point, you make a test outline that is strictly for the material that will be covered on this test. My test outlines were always one page and usually very brief. You do not need to go into any detail at this point. Your test outline is a part of your first overview.

Include main topics that are covered in as brief a manner as is reasonable. For example, if your upcoming test covers Shakespeare's play, *A Midsummer Night's Dream*, your test outline might start out looking something like this:

> *A Midsummer Night's Dream*
>> Characters
>> Plot
>> Conflict
>> Resolution or Conclusion

If you notice something special in your class notes (perhaps one of those items where the professor said, "Now pay close attention to this point"), you should include a reference to it in your test outline.

Understand that this outline will change and grow as you do a more detailed study of your notes and your materials. You are creating a good study tool that is based on the material on which you are being tested.

You now have a good idea of what is going to be on the test and what you need to study. As previously stated, this knowledge greatly weakens the greatest stress producer—fear of the unknown. You now know, more or less, what material will be on your test.

Second Overview, in Detail, Noting Strengths and Weaknesses

Your daily review gives you the basic knowledge that you need for this test, and your overview gives you a good, general idea of what will be on the test. Your next step is to begin to flesh out your test outline in more detail with the material from your daily review, class notes, quizzes, etc. This time overview is probably not the right word, but it does encompass the idea that you will need to look at everything, only this time it will be in more detail.

"Do not allow your pride or the embarrassment of having to ask for assistance stop you from getting whatever help you need."

I suggest you interlineate your test outlines with enough detail to help you recall the material. Creating your own paraphrases is a wonderful way to complete this second, more detailed overview. You need not be so detailed that you end up totally rewriting your notes. Simply write enough in your test outline so that you know which materials you are referring to. The very act of writing the outline will make you handle the material again, further reinforcing your knowledge of it.

While completing this second overview, pay special attention to any weaknesses you have. As you plug information from your daily notes into your test outline, make a mark in the margin of your outline any time you are unsure of the material. Don't let it upset you when you discover that, despite daily reviews and having a methodical approach to studying, you still have some gaps in your knowledge. The reason you review for a test is to be sure there are no gaps. This step in your test preparation has done its job. It has helped to solidify your knowledge and pointed out the weaknesses in your understanding of the material.

After you have completed your test outline as suggested above, you will have a fair idea of what will be on your test, and you will also know where your weak points are.

You now must go back to those areas where you noted your weaknesses to shore up your knowledge. Perhaps all you will need to do is re-read a section of your text. You may need to consult your professor or a classmate. At this point, you have invested a fair amount of time and energy into this test. Do not allow your pride or the embarrassment of having to ask for assistance stop you from getting whatever help you need. Make sure that there are no more weak areas in your knowledge before you move on from the Second Overview in Detail.

Your test outline now likely looks like a scribbled mess. That's okay. Since this is the outline you will use for most of your studying, you might want to recopy it to make it more legible. It's up to you. I sometimes recopied my test outline and other times made do with my messy marked-up version. Either way, the important thing is that you have now created a master document from which to study.

Most of what we do in education and commerce today is on the computer. We don't use pencil and paper very much anymore. Studying is the exception. Learn to do your test outline long hand. It is a much more organic means of handling the material. I also recommend taking notes in class the same way—long hand. This also has the added benefit of lessening the distractions of online social media.

You must now invest the time necessary to ensure that you own this material. Recite, from memory, what you know about the material. Use your test outline as a prompt, point by point, and recall the material as it appears in your notes. If you need to verify a point that is unclear, you can always turn to your daily notes or other study materials. Your test outline is your test template. You are using it to help you recall and learn all you need for this test.

Now that you have shored up your knowledge in your weak areas and have invested ample time into learning the material for this test, you are ready for your final review.

Final Review

At this point, use everything at your disposal to study. Your main tool is your test outline, no matter how battered and interlineated it is by now. Read over your class notes, one page at a time. Certain pages will be so familiar by now that it will take very little time to recite the material.

Do the same with your returned homework and quizzes, always returning to your test outline to be sure that you understand how all this material fits into the big picture.

Some materials simply need repetition, such as conjugating verbs in a foreign language. Other materials are best mastered by continuing to work practice problems, such as for math-intensive classes where you are working with formulas and numbers. The subject matter of your test will determine how you carry out your final review. I have included what I believe are a few general principles to guide you through your final review.

Don't Leave Anything to Chance

First, don't leave anything to chance. You should never assume that you will remember a particular point. Test your recall by making yourself repeat (aloud is best) those areas with which you are struggling. You are not finished with your final review until you can adequately recite every item on which you expect to be tested.

> *"Without regular reviewing, you will end up going from crisis to crisis . . ."*

Your upcoming test is your chance to shine, to show what you have learned. This test is only one test, but it is an integral part of your semester's grade in this one class, which in turn makes up a portion of your semester's class load. Remember always to think globally when it comes to your education. Every test is one more building block. Every test is another chance to succeed. Don't leave your success to chance. Invest the time that it takes to succeed on this test.

Nothing Beats Repetition

Second, nothing beats repetition for substantial amounts of material. By going over material repeatedly, you create neural pathways in your brain that are connecting and making a "home" for the material. But be careful—if you are simply staring at the material without truly grasping it, you are only wasting time. Here is a good trick to ensure that you are truly "getting it" and not just spinning your wheels.

Take your hand and cover the preceeding paragraph. Now, without peeking, repeat the main theme of the previous paragraph. Good. Most of you can do this without too much trouble. Now (still no peeking), recite the two main supporting points of the paragraph in your own words. Some of you are having a little more trouble with this part. This is an effective way to test yourself as you are going through your notes. Either use a piece of paper or your hand to cover one section at a time. Next, try the same exercise with each page of your class notes. You will be amazed at how much you can recite when you put yourself to the task.

Don't Try to Outguess the Professor

Third, don't try to outguess the professor. Don't be a person who tries to study enough to "get by." This will ultimately come back to haunt you. The professor has likely given you enough clues that you need not try to outguess him or her. Trying to guess the pinpoint areas on which your professor will test you takes two things: time and luck. Don't waste your time in this way, and don't trust your academic future to luck. Don't try to shortcut the demanding work of being a student. Study as if your life depended on it.

Mnemonics, Associations, and Anagrams

Fourth, use mnemonics, associations, or other memory strategies to help you remember substantial amounts of material. My suggestion is to create whatever anagrams or mnemonics to which the materials lend themselves. I referenced study aids on page **73**. We will go into more detail here. Be creative when inventing study aids. Use whatever assists you in your style of learning.

A mnemonic is an association system that assists you in learning. Matteo Ricci, a Jesuit missionary to China in the sixteenth century, invented a system of memorization that used the association of a familiar building and its contents to assist his students in learning new material. The new material would be mentally "attached" to a particular room in the house (in Ricci's time, it was a castle). The student would mentally picture the room as a general place and associate the room with a general topic. Specific information would then be further associated with specific items in the room. The idea is to be able to take a mental stroll through familiar rooms of familiar surroundings and associate these familiar items and settings with new material. When the student would "walk" from one room to the next, she would not have to worry about forgetting the newly learned material because she could always return to the familiar room and the associations would still be there.

This system takes some practice, but it assisted me greatly in my graduate studies. If you are interested in learning more about Ricci's system, I recommend reading Castles in the Air by Matteo Ricci.

Associations can be useful, but they may also be time consuming. The ones that pop into your mind because the new and old items are so similar are the ones that will likely help you the most. There is already a similar neural pathway to the one you are trying to create, and your mind found the pathway and bubbled it up to the surface on its own.

Anagrams take the first one or two letters of a word and make a new word using these letters. Most of us learned ROYGBIV for the colors of the rainbow and Every Good Boy Does Fine for the five lines of the treble clef staff in music. Anagrams are very useful for recalling a considerable amount of information. Use these to recall lists of characters or places or elements. To create an anagram, take the first letter of each word that you must remember and create a word from it. For example, if I needed to recall for my test the names of all of Caesar's friends in Shakespeare's work, *Anthony and Cleopatra*, my list would look like this:
(see next page)

Maecenas
Agrippa
Dolabella
Proculeius
Thidias
Gallus

My anagram, therefore, would include the letters M, A, D, P, T, and G. My anagram might be "mad p-t-g", or it may be "map d-t-g." Either of these would help me recall the names. You can also go outside of the first letter. For example, as long as you remember that there are no letter O's in your cast of characters, your anagram might be "am top dog." You would simply remove the "o's" to get the letters you need to create the anagram. This can be a fun way of recalling a great deal of information.

One word of caution about using anagrams. You should only put together your anagrams after you are somewhat familiar with the material. No amount of study tricks will replace a routine of studying, reviewing, and learning. Recalling, by use of an anagram, the word "am top dog" without knowing the material well enough to be able to recall whose name begins with a G is useless. Applying an anagram is strictly a test-taking technique that helps you recall the information that you have already mastered.

One of the biggest mistakes students make is purchasing books to help them study for specific tests without having acquired the basic study habits they need to profit from these books. They want a book to help them over the hurdle of a test without mastering the material. Test-taking techniques have limits as to how much they can help you. You must first master the material and then—and only then—apply these techniques to help you recall the material in an organized manner.

Stay Focused

Fifth, stay focused on the test at hand. Remember that you only have one test in your entire academic career—the next one! Don't allow other tests or other assignments crowd into your study time for this test. Imagine a baseball player at the plate, ready at bat to begin in the game, thinking to himself, "Gee, I hope I can execute a suicide squeeze bunt to win the game in the ninth inning." That would be ridiculous! The first pitch hasn't been thrown, and he is worrying about a play that is nine innings away! Worrying about other homework or tests at this point is a distraction and a time waster.

You have a much better chance of success if you stay focused on the task at hand. This is true not only of test taking but of life in general. Most of us do our best when we concentrate our efforts on one task at a time.

Performing Well on Your Test;
Don't Reinvent the Wheel

Sixth, keep it simple. Don't try to reinvent the wheel when answering test questions. Just give the professor what he or she asks for on the test. A test is the wrong place to try out your pet theory, or to continue a running argument that you have with your professor. You can argue policy or opposing theories of life later. Use your test to prove how much you know and how well you have mastered the material at hand.

Your final review could include all these test-taking ideas or only one or two of them. You might create helpful memory devices of your own as you study your test outline or other materials. That's great! The point is, this is your final review before the test. Make sure you get everything possible from your final review.

Timing Isn't Everything, but It's Important

A few final words on the timing of studying for a test. If possible, make your initial review at least one full day before your second overview when you begin to flesh out your test outline. You want to be a little more familiar with the material from the first overview before you begin to try to add detail to your test outline.Try to accomplish the various steps of reviewing on successive days, sometimes leaving a day of repetition for a step, if the test material and weight of the test call for it.

NEVER leave your final review for the day of the exam. Your final, comprehensive review should ideally be the day before the test. On the day of the test, don't feel that you must repeat, one final time, everything you have gone over up until then. Considering how comprehensive your review has been to this point, it likely would not be possible to repeat all of your preparation.

If you feel you must review on the day of the test, be sure that you are on track to get your butterflies to fly in formation. Use your test outline. Let it be your security blanket!

Make sure you get a good night's sleep the night before the exam. This is a point that is often lost on students. A friend of mine who was a top student in my class received a near-failing grade on a very important exam. Totally dismayed, this student went to the professor to retrieve the test booklet to review the answers. The problem was clear immediately: the exam was almost completely illegible. This student had stayed up for forty-eight hours studying prior to the exam. Two hours of focused writing looked like the scribbles of a four-year-old. Sleep deprivation was this student's undoing. Don't repeat this mistake. Get a good night's sleep.

Post-mortem

Finally, I suggest you do a brief post-mortem on each of your tests to gauge how well your preparation matched the actual test. By a post-mortem, I mean that no matter what grade you received, once the test is handed back to you, you should take out your test outline and your returned test and compare the two. What did you include on your test outline that was not on your test? What was on your test that was missing from your outline? What was on your outline that you still did not get correct on the test? Answering these questions can be very instructive.

Perhaps you were too detailed and spent too much time with fine points that were not tested. Perhaps it was the opposite: your test outline was too general and you did not do well because of your lack of details. Taking time to go over the test to see where you could have improved your test outline will be the first positive step for the next test you have to take!

> *"One of the biggest mistakes students make is purchasing books to help them study for specific tests without having acquired the basic study habits they need to profit from these books."*

Don't neglect this step if you did well on a test. You can gain some great insights into your reviewing procedures by comparing how you prepared with how you fared on each test. This is especially true when you do not do as well as you had hoped.

Remember, tests are the FUN part of your education.

MARK A. MATEYA, ESQ.

Self Assessment

Self Assessment

In order to be better prepared for the rest of your tests throughout your college career, take this self-assessment test on your test preparation routine. There are three questions you should ask yourself to begin your test preparation. They are:

How well   ?

How much   ?

How much   ?

There are five components surrounding tests and test preparation.

They are:

1.

2.

3.

4.

5.

Complete this sentence.

During my entire academic career, I only have one test...

CHAPTER 7

Finals

Studying for Finals:
Where Should I Begin?
Steps to Preparing for a Final

"Every mental pursuit
takes its reality and
worth from the ardour
of the pursuer."
John Keats

Finals deserve more attention and greater focus than normal tests. They are often what distinguishes good students from great students. I can hear some of you saying, "But I thought you said not to get too stressed out about tests!" Yes, it's true that you should keep your education in perspective, but as educational events go, finals rank at the very top. This is where the best students prove themselves.

It is up to you to learn just how much weight each of your finals is worth. If your final is weighted the same as all the other tests during the semester, then you need to put in only as much time and effort as it took for you to master the material and to get an A on your earlier tests. If, however, your final is weighted as a higher percentage of your grade than your normal tests, then give it more time and attention.

You should employ the strategies from "Steps to Preparing for a Test" (see page 83) for your finals. In this chapter, I have made only those additions or changes that address finals.

One point that remains the same is the fun factor. Not fun as in Disney World fun, but fun as in a sense of accomplishment and satisfaction. This is your big chance to shine! The sense of doing your absolute best on a final is something that screams self-fulfillment like few other experiences. Make the most of this great opportunity, as you will only have one final for each class.

Studying for Finals . . . When Should I Begin?

Unlike tests, you cannot wait until three or four days before your final exam to begin studying and expect to do reasonably well. Finals require more time, as you will likely be covering anywhere from one-half to a full semester's worth of material.

Since you will require more time to study, I recommend that you schedule your studying time as soon as you get your class syllabus for the semester. If you see that your final is on Thursday, May 14th, you should schedule review sessions for that final beginning ten days to two weeks ahead of time, depending upon your other finals and class assignments that will be due. Don't wait until five days before finals week to sit down and decide when you are going to study for finals. At that point it's called crisis management! Heaven help you if you have not been reviewing your notes daily.

"Taking time to go over the test to see where you could have improved your test outline will be the first positive step for the next test you have to take!"

Some people like studying for hours at a time while others can only work for one hour before they need a ten-minute break. I know that I fall into the latter category and require a breather. My eyes get too tired if I read for too long. Because of this, I need to schedule longer study periods, as there is a higher percentage of my time taken up with breaks.

Whatever works for your style of studying and reading, be sure to schedule your time accordingly.

You should begin studying one week prior to your final at the absolute latest! Make this your deadline, so that if your test is on the fourteenth, you will begin studying no later than the seventh. This may give you enough time to be thorough and to go back and fill in any blanks that you may still have in your knowledge.

Steps to Preparing for a Final

Daily Review

At this point I sound like a broken record. Your daily review, along with your class notes and your three-ring binder, are still the backbone of your knowledge in any given class. Nothing new here!

First Overview

Your first overview will be similar to the one you did for a test, only here you will not limit yourself to a single page test outline. *Your final outline, which you will create during your first overview, should be based on your earlier test outlines plus anything that you have gleaned from your post-mortems and anything to which your professor has told you to pay particular attention.* You have already been tested at least once, sometimes more than once, on most of the material that goes into your final outline. For this reason, your final outline can be fairly detailed right from the start.

You should immediately note any areas in which you know you are weak. Don't wait for your second review: this time you must solidify your knowledge more quickly because you have more to cover.

This first overview must include more than just your daily class notes. It should include your textbook, handouts, homework, quizzes, and any other information that you have picked up through the entire semester that may show up on your final. Your final outline will be complete only after you have reviewed each page of these materials and noted any weak spots or gaps in your knowledge.

There is nothing sweeter, academically, than acing a final! Create a good final outline and you are on your way!

Studying from the Final Outline

Use your final outline to study for your final, as it already contains a fair amount of detail. You can add in another quick perusal of your class notes on any other material that will add to your overall understanding of the material.

You should review for your final the same way you would for a test, only be a little harder on yourself. Don't let yourself off the hook. Take responsibility for your own education at this level. You will be paid incredible dividends, not only on this final, but also on all your academic endeavors.

Be sure to understand each portion of the material thoroughly before you move on to studying and reciting the next section. Go through each main topic, each supporting point, and each unique piece of information that you have gathered. This is your time to stay focused, not to let up, and to take advantage of all your preparation. When studying for finals, you need to take your review to another level. One way you can do this is to write out simple overview statements for each heading of your final outline. Once you have mastered all the headings and main topics, go back and do the same thing for each of the supporting facts. This will take some time but will pay off

Outline Example
Title of Outline
I. Main topic
   A. Subtopic that gives more information about main topic I.
      1. Detail that gives more info about subtopic A.
      2. Detail for subtopic A.
   B. Subtopic for main idea I.
      1. Detail for subtopic B.
      2. Detail for subtopic B.
II. Main topic
   A. Subtopic that gives more information about main topic II.
      1. Detail that gives more info about subtopic A.
      2. Detail for subtopic A.
   B. Subtopic for main idea II.
      1. Detail for subtopic B.
      2. Detail for subtopic B.
III. Main topic
   A. Subtopic that gives more information about main topic III.
      1. Detail that gives more info about subtopic A.
         a. Detail for detail 1
         b. Detail for detail 1
      2. Detail for subtopic A.
   B. Subtopic for main idea III.
      1. Detail for subtopic B.
      2. Detail for subtopic B.

during the test. You may also be surprised to see how your daily review has prepared you for this final. Much of this information will be nearly second nature by now.

Another good test preparation tip is to write out a brief outline of all the material that will be on this final from memory. Use your test outline to prompt you if necessary. By having to write out the material in outline form, you are forcing yourself to synthesize the material into an organized framework that you can handle. You are making it your own! And I again suggest that you do all of this writing in long hand.

This second step in reviewing for your final can take you as few as two to three days or as many as five to ten days. I've given you two effective ways to review for your test. You will, undoubtedly, come up with variations of your own. Do whatever you must in order to master the material.

How will you know when you have reviewed enough? I'm not sure there is an easy answer to that question. As stated in the previous chapter, you cannot cut corners. You must be thorough and hold yourself up to a high standard by using what I call positive self-control. It is called "self" control because you are the self in control, and no one else can do for you what you alone can do. God made us this way. I am using the phrase "self-control" in a positive manner, meaning that you decide what transpires, no one else. Use self-control to push yourself to do your very best. Don't let up until you are as prepared as you can be. You can do it!

Final Review

Your final review of your test outline and other materials should be a breeze. Your second step of studying from your final outline has given you a mastery of the material that only comes from spending time and energy on the material. Once you have mastered the material at the second step, your final review is to test yourself.

In order to test yourself, have someone quiz you on the material. A classmate who is studying the same material should ideally do the quizzing. Lacking a classmate, your quizmaster should be someone who is at least familiar with the material in the general sense. It will make the quizzing more useful and will keep it moving more quickly. If no one is available to assist you, you can quiz yourself by covering your final outline, one section at a time, and reciting the material. This final review via quizzing should be done one or two days before the final.

This final quiz should be line by line through your study materials, in the same order as your class notes this first time through. You learned it in that order and, therefore, recalling it in that order will further reinforce it for you.

When you are answering these questions, keep your hands off your (well-worn by now) three-ring binder and answer the questions as succinctly, yet accurately, as possible. Don't interrupt the quizzing to review an answer should you happen to get an answer wrong. When you miss a question, write it down and move on to the next question. Go back and re-review those areas that you missed all at once. Once you have corrected your errors to your satisfaction, repeat the final review quiz.

The second time through this final quiz, the questions should be in random order, not in the order of your notes. This makes you dig a little deeper. You will find you can recall the material even when it is in a different order than your notes. It may simply take a little longer. Your mind must go through the notes to "find" the information. If you fail to take this second step of quizzing yourself out of order, then the very first time you try to recall the information out of order will be on your final exam. THAT is not a very good idea.

If you have answered everything accurately on your second review quiz, you are ready for your final. Congratulations! If not, go back and complete another review. You will reach a plateau where you will be comfortable with your level of understanding of the material. Stop there. At this point, you are probably one day prior to your final. Now you need only to *maintain*.

Maintain this level by going over your notes, page by page, to keep yourself familiar with what you have built into your memory. Don't overdo it. Go over your notes just enough to keep from being nervous.

Be sure to get a good night's sleep before the final. Don't try to learn new material at this point, as there is no time to integrate the new material into the large framework you have created. Trying to add new material at this point can confuse you. This is often what happens to students who cram for finals. Some of them are lucky enough to do passably well, but it is not an effective way for a serious student to study. And the student who crams in information rarely retains it for long. His education is cheapened by his own actions.

> "Write out a brief outline of all the material that will be on this final from memory."

After you have thoroughly studied for a final, you don't want to confuse yourself by trying to distinguish the finest of fine points. Guard against straining at micro bits of information. Remember, you do NOT want to be a nitpicker! Don't do anything at this point that could confuse the mastery of the material that you have attained.

Your ability to answer questions on your final review quizzes should convince you that you are ready for the final. There is no longer any reason for fear of the unknown. You know the material and are now free to have fun on your final by showing how much you know!

Self Assessment

Finals are the testing ground that separates the wheat from the chaff, the silver from the dross, the, well, you get the idea. To assist you with finals preparation, take this self assessment test.

• Going over all your materials, page by page, shows that you are:

    a) anal retentive and wound too tightly.

    b) doing your best to prepare for your final.

    c) mindlessly following all the instructions you read in any book.

    d) not a big believer in the 'random guessing test-taking system' used by so many college students today.

• To do my best on my finals this year, I will begin studying at least _____ days prior to my finals.

• While reviewing your test outline you come across information that you swear you never heard before. You should:

    a) ignore it.

    b) convince yourself that if you don't remember it, surely your professor won't remember it either.

    c) dig a little deeper and find out what it is all about.

    d) hope like the dickens that it won't be on the test.

• The_____is the most critical part of my study routine.

CHAPTER 8

Checklists

When Should I Use a Checklist?
What Should My Checklist Include?
How Do I Make a Personalized Checklist?

"Some know the value of education by having it. I know its value by not having it."
Frederick Douglas

I n this chapter I want to briefly cover using checklists as an additional safety net. You can use a checklist in addition to your final outline or your test outline. I am offering them as an alternative tool that you can use at any point in your academic work. A thorough checklist will assist you in making sure that you have done everything you need to do for an assignment, a class, or a semester.

Why Use Checklists?

You may be asking, "Why add one more thing? I'm already following your suggestions that ensure that I have double- and triple-checked everything from my notes to my outlines." Checklists can be an additional line of defense against letting some assignment or some important piece of information slip between the cracks. Checklists are best if you do them by hand yourself, as this requires you to handle the information yourself one moretime.

Once you see how simple it is to use checklists, you will likely be encouraging your fellow students to use them as well.

When Should I Use a Checklist?

You can use a checklist to assist you in completing a paper or project, in studying for a test, or studying for a final. You can create a checklist to help you remember what you need to get done by Wednesday night so that you are free to take Thursday off

105

from your regular studies to attend the opera or the roller derby. You employ a checklist whenever you cannot afford to forget _____(you fill in the blank).

What Should My Checklist Include?

Only the essentials need to go in your checklist. It is somewhere between your Preliminary overview and your Detailed Overview for a test in scope. Include anything that must not be forgotten.

If, for example, you were writing a research paper or essay, you might include things like:

- ☐ Rough draft from outline
- ☐ Begin research
- ☐ Note my sources
- ☐ Revise outline, if necessary
- ☐ Second draft, with new sources
- ☐ Check spelling and grammar
- ☐ Double-check sources, if necessary
- ☐ Prepare bibliography (or whatever verification necessary)
- ☐ Final draft
- ☐ Final proofread

This checklist then stays with the essay until it is completed. I have not added anything **extraneous** to the project. I simply organized the process, from top to bottom.

Once you have created your checklist (which usually only takes one or two minutes), you can transfer each item to your calendar if you like. It's up to you.

The great advantage of using a checklist is that it can alert you when you are falling short. For example, if you are just a few days away from the date you are to hand in your essay and you notice that you have not double-checked your sources, you know that you must do so before you proceed any further.

How Do I Make a Personalized Checklist?

You already know what is important in each class or project. If your instruction for an essay is to do traditional research plus do an interview of at least one professional who can comment on your topic, then you include "Interview professional for comment" on your checklist. It truly is that simple. It requires a little creativity and a desire to do thorough work to create a very useful checklist.

Don't overthink this process. You may be able to succeed without checklists, or you may have an alternative to using checklists. Great! My goal here, as with this entire book, is to assist you in getting all you can from your education. If you do not need checklists to complete projects or assignments—fine. Just keep the idea in the back of your mind. You might need it one day.

CHAPTER 9

Technology in Studying

" Technology is just a tool."
Bill Gates

Technology offers information at our fingertips at lightning speed. We can retrieve almost anything we need with a few clicks of a button. Ipads, handheld devices, and smart phones are all great. They make our lives easier. The marketing that surrounds these data-driven devices suggests that "there is an app for everything." Studying is different.

Studying is a constant. No matter how much technology improves, each of us must master the art of studying our material so that we make the material our own. The fact that we can Google, download, and then cut-and-paste nearly any information does not replace studying. Locating very good, pin-pointed information is not the same as studying information and making it your own.

While technology and e-books have supplanted everything from cookbooks to sheet music, colleges report that paper textbooks are still the chosen medium for the vast majority of professors and students. Use technology to your advantage, by all means. But don't think technology will replace your need to do the hard work of studying. Being able to access any information on your handheld device does not replace your needing to learn it and integrate it into your own life. Total recall has a limit.

I stated earlier that I had an acquaintance in school who had a photographic memory. He could recall anything. That gave him an advantage, but it did not replace the work of studying the material. He failed to work with his own intellect and reasoning or apply his own thoughts to the material. Initially, he tried to replace studying with his "total recall" of material and he nearly failed out of school. He had to learn this new skill: studying.

Using handheld devices or laptops in the classroom is common. Many students will rely on these to prepare for class and take notes during class.

"Studying is a learned skill."

The idea of using a notebook and a pencil seems very old-fashioned. I understand that. This system of note taking, creating study outlines, and going through daily repetition is designed to help you learn how to succeed academically. Remember, the daily review is the backbone of your study routine. None of this lines up with the "cut-and-paste" way of thinking. It is not easy. It is hard work, but it is worth it.

I like comparing my system of note taking—using study outlines and daily repetition—to Dave Ramsey's Financial Peace University program. Dave teaches his students how to succeed with money by using a tried-and-true system of budgeting every dollar on paper before the month begins (a zero-based budget). He then teaches the baby steps of having a starter emergency fund, paying off all of your debts smallest to largest (including student loans), before fully funding your emergency fund, and then saving for college (for your children) and retirement before paying off your mortgage and becoming very generous to others.

Dave Ramsey is fond of saying, "We give you the same advice your grandmother gave you" as a way of identifying his financial system as a basic, commonsense way of succeeding with money. Achieving

Academic Excellence; How to Study is much the same. It is applying basic skills in a specific manner to achieve the best results possible.

The skills you learn and put to use here, with paper and pencil, will be useful to you in whatever career path you choose. You are learning how to learn when you apply these principles. Notice the first sentence of this paragraph: "The skills you learn and put to use" will be of great benefit to you. Let me expound on that idea in a way that I hope will motivate you to do the hard work of learning how to study. I want to give you a few examples, at least one of which hopefully resonate with you.

Compound interest is amazing. Albert Einstein called compound interest the "eighth wonder of the world." We all know that saving money is a good idea, but few of us do it. If you saved just $30 a month in a good mutual fund for 12 years, you would have contributed about $4,350. Your money, however, would actually be worth $9,360, more than double what you saved in just 12 years (the time it took you to graduate from high school). Just knowing about compound interest doesn't help you if you don't apply the knowledge and save money.

Smoking kills people every year by causing various types of cancer, predominantly lung cancer. Approximately 15% of Americans still smoke – slightly more than that in the 18- to 24-year-old range. So knowing that smoking can be deadly does not change the behavior of at least 15 out of 100 of us. Our actions have to follow the lead of what our minds tell us.

One more example.

Texting while driving causes car accidents. We know we shouldn't do it, but too many of us are still texting "just this one thing" while we drive our cars. Simply having this information (i.e., downloading it, reading about it on Facebook) is not enough. I could give more examples of eating healthy foods, exercising, getting enough sleep and taking care of your health, generally. I trust you will see what this chapter (and this book) is all about. It is about you wanting to succeed enough to change your behavior. Knowing what to do and doing it are two separate things.

You are the only one who can change your behavior. Learning how to study and making the most of your academic career is modifying your behavior. This doesn't mean that if you do everything that I recommend you will soar to the top of your class and get straight As. But it does mean that you will do your best. You will be the best student that you can be.

We each have varying degrees of talent and ability. We are responsible to be our best and do the best we can with what God has given us. Studying is a learned skill. We can learn how to study – and there are many books like this one that teach marvelous tricks and tips on how to study and take notes and prepare for tests. However, purchasing all those books and downloading all those ideas will not make you a better student any more than reading about investments without actually putting your money into an investment account would make you a millionaire. You have to do the work! You have to amend your old ways and adopt new ones.

We are each given the same number of hours in a day. Some of us produce works of art. Some of us are lazy and think someone else owes us an income. Some of us work outside the home and others are stay-at-home parents, caring for their families. We decide what we will do with the 24 hours we are given each day. If you are a student, your job is to get the best grades you can. Your job is to succeed at being a student. Learning these study skills will help you make the most of your academic career.

Happy Studying. May God bless your efforts.

MARK A. MATEYA, ESQ.

Illustration Credits:

http://etc.usf.edu
https://free.clipartof.com
https://www.vecteezy.com

Index